BRYAN FAMILY

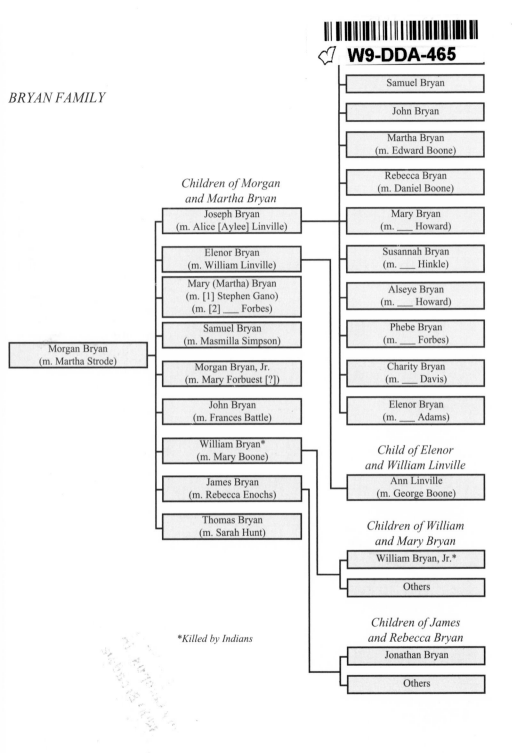

Children of Morgan
and Martha Bryan

Samuel Bryan

John Bryan

Martha Bryan
(m. Edward Boone)

Rebecca Bryan
(m. Daniel Boone)

Joseph Bryan
(m. Alice [Aylee] Linville)

Mary Bryan
(m. ___ Howard)

Elenor Bryan
(m. William Linville)

Susannah Bryan
(m. ___ Hinkle)

Mary (Martha) Bryan
(m. [1] Stephen Gano)
(m. [2] ___ Forbes)

Alseye Bryan
(m. ___ Howard)

Samuel Bryan
(m. Masmilla Simpson)

Phebe Bryan
(m. ___ Forbes)

Morgan Bryan
(m. Martha Strode)

Morgan Bryan, Jr.
(m. Mary Forbuest [?])

Charity Bryan
(m. ___ Davis)

John Bryan
(m. Frances Battle)

Elenor Bryan
(m. ___ Adams)

William Bryan*
(m. Mary Boone)

Child of Elenor
and William Linville

James Bryan
(m. Rebecca Enochs)

Ann Linville
(m. George Boone)

Thomas Bryan
(m. Sarah Hunt)

Children of William
and Mary Bryan

William Bryan, Jr.*

Others

*Killed by Indians

Children of James
and Rebecca Bryan

Jonathan Bryan

Others

My Father,
Daniel Boone

My Father, Daniel Boone

(G)

The Draper Interviews with Nathan Boone

Edited by Neal O. Hammon

With an Introduction
by Nelson L. Dawson

THE UNIVERSITY PRESS OF KENTUCKY

Publication of this volume was made possible in part by a grant
from the E.O. Robinson Mountain Fund and the
National Endowment for the Humanities.

Scholarly publisher for the Commonwealth,
serving Bellarmine College, Berea College, Centre College of Kentucky,
Eastern Kentucky University, The Filson Club Historical Society,
Georgetown College, Kentucky Historical Society, Kentucky State University,
Morehead State University, Murray State University, Northern Kentucky
University, Transylvania University, University of Kentucky,
University of Louisville, and Western Kentucky University.

Editorial and Sales Offices: The University Press of Kentucky
663 South Limestone Street, Lexington, Kentucky 40508-4008

99 00 01 02 03   5 4 3 2

Frontispiece:
Nathan Boone. Courtesy of the Missouri Historical Society, St. Louis.

Library of Congress Cataloging-in-Publication Data
Boone, Nathan, 1781-1856
My father, Daniel Boone : the Draper interviews with Nathan Boone /
edited by Neal O. Hammon ; with an introduction by Nelson L. Dawson.
p.   cm.
Lyman Draper's 1851 interviews with Nathan and Olive Boone.
Includes bibliographical references and index.
ISBN 0-8131-2103-5 (cloth : alk. paper)
1. Boone, Daniel, 1734-1820. 2. Pioneers—Kentucky—Biography.
3. Frontier and pioneer life—Kentucky. 4. Kentucky—Biography. 5. Boone, Nathan,
1781-1856—Interviews. 6. Boone, Olive Van Bibber, 1783-1858—Interviews.
I. Boone, Olive Van Bibber, 1783-1858. II. Draper, Lyman Copeland, 1815-1891.
III. Hammon, Neal O. IV. Title.
F454.B66B66   1999
976.9'02'092—dc21
[b]   99-19263

This book is printed on acid-free recycled paper meeting the requirements of the
American National Standard for Permanence of Paper for Printed Library Materials.

To my father,
Stratton O. Hammon

CONTENTS

Maps and Illustrations

PREFACE

Research on the life of Daniel Boone would not be complete without his biographies. One of the more reliable accounts is the recent work of John Mack Faragher, *Daniel Boone: The Life and Legend of an American Pioneer* (New York, 1992). Mr. Faragher was clever enough to steer clear of some controversial subjects, such as Boone's alleged visit to Harrodsburg in 1774.

It is easy to see that John Bakeless spent a great deal of time on research for his biography, *Daniel Boone* (New York, 1939). His work was the model for several later versions, including Lawrence Elliott's *The Long Hunter: A New Life of Daniel Boone* (New York, 1976) and Michael A. Lofaro's *The Life and Adventures of Daniel Boone* (Lexington, 1978). The other biographies published before Bakeless's offer much fiction but few facts regarding Boone's life.

The noted exception is the first, the alleged autobiography contained in John Filson's *The Discovery, Settlement and Present State of Kentucke* (Wilmington, 1784). In his interview with Lyman Draper, Nathan Boone criticizes Filson's style and vocabulary, but he does not fault the facts. In my research I have discovered only one important typographical error made by Filson (or his printer): Filson's book records 6 June as the date that Daniel Boone left Castlewood to search for the surveyors in 1774, whereas Boone, in a later deposition, gives 26 June as the date.

In Nathan's account, the readers must decide what is the truth. I have attempted to keep the text as accurate as possible and have added brackets and footnotes to assist the readers, but I have not changed any of the facts mentioned in the interview.

In editing Draper's interview with Nathan Boone it soon became obvious that some word and sentence structures needed to be modified slightly to accomodate modern readers. Added information, such as first names or words used for clarification, was placed in brackets. Draper was not always consistent with his spelling; for example, both *Stewart* and *Stuart* are used in the original, and like many other historians, he uses both *Boonesboro* and *Boonesborough*. Here the word choice is that most often used in the original. I also found some of Nathan's remembrances were chronologically out of order and needed to be reorganized.

For the historians, the page numbers of Draper's notes are interspersed throughout the text to make it easier to correlate with the original. The entire work is included in pages 19 through 294 of file 6S of the Draper manuscript, which simplifies research of the subject.

Only a small amount of the original manuscript has been omitted. The omitted material, mostly detailed information on the Bryan family and the career of Nathan Boone after his father's death, is contained in pages 6S282 through 6S294 of Draper's notes. However, not all the material was omitted; some paragraphs from these pages were inserted chronologically into the printed text or used in the introduction.

Prior to this interview, Draper wrote Nathan Boone, asking him seventeen questions about his father. Boone's answer to the letter can be found within Draper file 6S as numbered pages 1 through 12. Upon arriving at Boone's dwelling, Draper also discovered a family genealogy, which he faithfully copied and included with the letter; the genealogical notes are included on pages 13 through 16 of the original. So that the reader might know all the facts available to Draper before the interview, Nathan's answers and the genealogy are appended to the text of this book.

A great deal of credit for this book is due to the work of my good friend Audrea McDowell. In 1975, her late husband, Robert Emmett McDowell Sr. was commissioned to write a biography of Daniel Boone. She assisted him by reviewing the Draper manuscripts on microfilm and typing portions onto cards. In 1995 Audrea let me use the cards and suggested that I publish any or all of the Draper notes. Her efforts saved me the time and trouble of recopying the material used in this book.

I would like to thank my dependable friend Nelson Dawson, the editor of the *Filson Club History Quarterly*, for writing the introduction. He also assisted in preparing the notes and bibliography.

Another friend, Richard Taylor, a talented writer and the proprietor of Poor Richard's Bookstore in Frankfort, Kentucky, lent me some of his books to research these notes. Then another friend, Ted Franklin Belue, also a writer and a Boone expert, suggested I contact Ken Kamper in Hopewell, Missouri. This proved to be good advice, since Kamper is a well-known Boone authority in that area and was very helpful. During my brief visit to Missouri, he directed me to all the original Spanish land grants of the Boone clan and provided pertinent information on family genealogy. Kemper also furnished much useful information about the original towns, dwellings, trails, and roads along the Missouri River.

In St. Louis I met with Ellen B. Thomasson, the Curatorial Assistant of Photographs and Prints for the Missouri Historical Society, who graciously provided material that was used for illustrations in this book. Likewise, I would like to thank Gayle L. Mooney, the Graphic Arts Specialist of the Missouri Department of Natural Resources, for furnishing the photograph of Nathan Boone's cabin at Ash Grove.

My wife, Barbara, was also very helpful, especially when I was doing research in St. Charles, Missouri. She managed to find some very excellent restaurants in that charming town.

INTRODUCTION

Daniel Boone is a unique American icon, the personification of that quintessential national hero, the frontiersman. He was already a figure of considerable fame in Kentucky in the 1770s, but John Filson's *The Adventures of Col. Daniel Boone,* published on Boone's fiftieth birthday in 1784, made him a figure of national, even international, renown.

Boone's stature, paradoxically, was largely unaffected by painful, repeated failure. His fortunes began to decline almost simultaneously with the end of the Revolutionary War and the publication of Filson's biography. Unsuccessful in business both as a merchant and as a speculator and by 1789 "unable to call a single acre . . . his own," Boone began a period of wandering. In 1799 he left Kentucky forever—or so he thought, not reckoning on the determination of the state he believed had spurned him to retrieve his remains from Missouri for reburial in Frankfort.

Boone is also a paradoxical American icon in that, despite his fame, he has remained a mystery; many of the things most people think they know about him are not true. The disjunction between myth and reality, to be sure not unknown in other American heroes, is particularly wide in Boone's case. In recent times we can blame television (always an inviting target) because of its wildly implausible *Daniel Boone* series (1964–1970) starring Fess Parker, but in fact the process had begun long before, indeed in Boone's own lifetime. Although he praised Filson's biographical treatment ("All true! Every word true! Not a lie in it!"), he became increasingly and ruefully aware of the mythmaking and was heard to comment on it more than once as an old man living out his days in Missouri.

So, then, who was he really, this American icon, this Daniel Boone?

Of course, there is no ready-made answer, and in the last analysis each of us, after weighing all the evidence, will have to decide for ourselves. But the information we need to make that decision is available almost entirely as a result of the tireless efforts of one unlikely man—Lyman Copeland Draper (1815–1891). Frail, scarcely five feet tall, weighing around one hundred pounds, Draper suffered from a number of health problems, some real and some imagined, for most of his adult life. Yet he traveled countless miles, collected thousands of manuscripts, interviewed the famous and obscure, and transformed the State Historical Society of Wisconsin into one of the leading state historical societies in the nation.

His life was dominated by three overpowering interests: history, religion (first the Baptists and then, after 1868, spiritualism), and the Democratic Party. Born in western New York, he heard many tales of the Revolutionary War and the War of 1812 from his father and his father's friends. By age sixteen he was already a collector, having requested and received a brief memoir from the venerable James Madison.

Peter Remsen, the husband of Draper's cousin Lydia (whom Draper later married) and a man of "spasmodic wealth," paid his way through Granville College in Ohio in the 1830s. After college Draper edited a Democratic newspaper in Mississippi, and when it failed, Remsen supported him while he collected historical material. Draper became nearly obsessed by the passing of the old frontiersman, and he determined to collect as much material and interview as many survivors as possible. He was particularly interested in material from the frontier (Virginia, Tennessee, Kentucky, and Ohio) from the period between 1763 and 1812.

In 1852 Draper moved to Wisconsin at the urging of Charles Larabee, an influential former classmate. The State Historical Society of Wisconsin was being formed at the time, and Larabee offered Draper the position of secretary with a salary of $600 a year and a $500-a-year acquisitions budget. Draper threw himself into his job with, if such a thing were possible, redoubled intensity. On one occasion during the Civil War, he visited Kentucky, seeking to rescue historical material from the flames of war, walking, the story goes, hundreds of miles after his transportation arrangements broke down. By the time Draper retired in 1886, he had achieved an amazing feat of historical collection. The library of the State Historical Society of Wisconsin grew from 50 vol-

Daniel Boone, portrait by Chester Harding. Courtesy of the Filson Club Historical Society.

umes in 1854 to 2,000 in 1855, 19,000 in 1864, 57,000 in 1874, and 110,000 in 1886. He bequeathed nearly 500 volumes of cataloged manuscripts to the society when he died in 1891.

Draper's lifework of collecting aroused resentment in some quarters. Reuben T. Durrett, the first president of the Filson Club Historical Society in Louisville, Kentucky, accused Draper of stealing documents and spiriting them away to Wisconsin, a charge that, while occasionally repeated by others, has no evidence to sustain it. The truth is quite otherwise; much material would have been lost forever were it not for Draper's efforts.

One story has it that Frederick Jackson Turner, whose seminal essay "The Significance of the Frontier in American History" (1893) launched his famous Frontier Thesis, once visited the elderly Draper and, after enduring hours of rambling discourse, came away vowing never to "fritter away any more time on the old dilettante." This tale, if true, would seem to reflect more unfavorably on Turner than on Draper, whose patient efforts over many years gathered the material on which Turner's work was based.

Other critics have pointed out that Draper, despite the wealth of historical material in his possession, was not able to develop an interpretive historical framework. He thought instinctively in terms of "dramatic history which celebrated heroic men and deeds" without any analysis of underlying causation. It is doubtful that Draper, whose main interests were in other areas of historical endeavor, would have understood the point of the criticism—nor, I must confess, do I.

George Orwell observed that every life is a failure as seen from within. While this may well be an overly grim assessment, it is true that Draper was haunted by a persistent sense of failure relating to his inability to write. He was obsessed with ambitious projects that never reached fruition because of a chronic case of writer's block. It is symptomatic that his one solid monograph, a study of the Battle of King's Mountain, appeared a year too late for the battle's centennial commemoration in 1883. His health always seemed adequate for arduous travel but deteriorated when he was alone in his study with pen in hand and sheet of blank paper before him. Not even his old friend Charles Larabee's "sarcasm and invective" could shame books from him.

Yet when all is said and done, we can see now that Draper, while the author of only a few works, was the father of many. And of these many works, a goodly number have dealt with Daniel Boone. Draper may not have had a head for theory, but he had an eye for a good story, particularly for one with an intriguing mixture of fact and legend.

Early in his career, therefore, Draper set about to explore the mystery of Daniel Boone. Of the four Boone children who were still living when Daniel died in 1820, only Nathan was still alive when Draper began his research. In 1842 Draper began a correspondence with Nathan, who with his wife Olive (Van Bibber) Boone lived in a large stone house in the Femme Osage Valley of St. Charles County, Missouri. In 1843 Draper made another significant contact with the Boone family when he began a correspondence with one of Boone's nephews, Daniel Boone Bryan of Lexington, Kentucky. In 1844 he had a long talk with Bryan and also acquired material from three of Squire Boone's sons, who introduced him to the considerable Boone family network in Kentucky and Missouri. Also in the 1840s he began visiting various Boone sites, making sketches and taking notes. In retrospect, however, it is clear that Nathan Boone was Draper's most important source for his Boone research.

Nathan Boone, though clearly overshadowed by his famous father, was nevertheless a significant figure in his own right. During the late 1820s the Nathan Boone family was one of the more prosperous families in the county, living well and entertaining lavishly. In the 1830s, however, Nathan began a restless stage of life that lasted until his retirement. He worked as a federal surveyor in Iowa, then joined the regular army and spent the next twenty years in distinguished service. He served in the Black Hawk War, explored the western plains, negotiated with Indians, patrolled the Sante Fe Trail, laid out military roads, and fought in the Mexican War. He retired near the age of seventy with the rank of lieutenant colonel. One of his contemporaries remembered him as "a remarkable woodsman who could climb like a bear and swim like a duck."

The family fortunes had declined in the 1830s, partly as a consequence of the Depression of 1837. During that year Nathan sold his home in St. Charles county, paid off some debts, and then built a "dog-trot" cabin in southwest Missouri on the headwaters of the Osage River, which was closer to his army postings in the West.

It was here that Draper came for a long visit in October and November of 1851, shortly after Nathan's retirement. Both Nathan and Olive had retentive memories, and Draper produced over three hundred pages of notes that constitute "the most important source for constructing the personal side of Daniel Boone's life." The importance of Draper's material can be gauged by studying the notes of Boone's biographies, particularly those of John Mack Faragher's *Daniel Boone: The Life and Legend of an American Pioneer* (1992). It is difficult to see how any but the sketchiest of Boone biographies could be written without the Draper material; time and time again, the Nathan Boone interview is cited on various aspects of Boone's personal life.

As Draper was preparing to leave, Nathan and Olive Boone gave him a small bundle of surviving Boone documents, including account books, survey and land records, and correspondence. It was an astonishingly successful visit, one that we now can see clearly was a landmark event in the history of Boone scholarship.

Draper never spoke to Nathan and Olive again. Nathan died in 1856 and Olive followed him two years later. They had, among other things, vastly expanded Draper's knowledge of the Boone genealogy; over the next forty years Draper contacted many of Boone's direct descendants and other kin in his ongoing research.

Even so, for Draper the very wealth of the Boone material became a source of intense vexation. Draper's chronic writer's block prevented completion of his long-projected and eagerly anticipated Boone biography. At his death he left a handwritten manuscript of several hundred pages that carried Boone's life only to the 1775 siege of Boonesborough. Toward the end of his arduous career, Draper wrote despairingly that he had "wasted my life in puttering." "When you are gone," a friend assured him, "the Historical Society of Wisconsin will be your monument more enduring than brass or marble." So it has proved to be.

And what of Daniel Boone himself? Each of us, inevitably, will see him somewhat differently. For me, the most striking and surprising result of a closer look at Boone is the way his sterling moral character shines steadily through all the vicissitudes of his remarkable life. Boone once wrote that "God never made a man of my principle to be lost." Indeed. My lasting impression of this baffling and perennially intriguing figure is that he was a good man who became a good old man, and a good old man, John Earle, the seventeenth-century English essayist tells us, "is the best antiquity."

Neal Hammon, a well-known Kentucky architect, is an amateur historian in the original meaning of this much-abused word (F. fr. L *amator* lover, fr. *amatus* pp. of amare to love). He loves Kentucky frontier history and during his lifetime of study has compiled an impressive bibliography of published works. We can be grateful to him for presenting Nathan Boone's reminiscences to us in this well-edited and richly annotated edition.

But it is past time to bring these preliminaries to an end, so that Nathan Boone, with his wife Olive's valuable help, can tell us about his father.

Nelson L. Dawson

1

HIS EARLY LIFE

Lyman Draper: Colonel Boone, what can you tell me about yourself and your father?

Nathan Boone: My name is Nathan Boone; I am the son of Colonel Daniel Boone. I was born at Boone Station, now Cross Plains, Fayette County, Kentucky, on March 21, 1781, and this is my wife, Olive Van Bibber Boone, the daughter of Peter Van Bibber, who was born in Greenbriar County, on the bank of Greenbriar River, on January 13, 1783, but when she was two years old, her father moved to Point Pleasant, West Virginia.

My father, Colonel Daniel Boone, used to say that his father, Squire Boone, and two brothers, or perhaps it might have been one brother and a sister, came to America on the same ship as William Penn, but not on the first nor last of Penn's visits to his colony, perhaps about 1699.[1]

Draper: No that would be too early, as your Grandfather Squire wasn't born until November 26, 1696.

Nathan Boone: Well, I would not know from my own knowledge, but I am telling you what my father heard from James Boone when he last visited his relatives in Berks County, Pennsylvania, in 1789. James was then an old bachelor and had been a schoolteacher. All the early Boones were Quakers. Father used to say that he knew of no other Boones in the country besides his own relatives.

Draper: This isn't exactly true, as I know of a Boone family in Maryland who are Catholics and who came over and settled before your family came to America.

Olive Boone: Regardless of when they came to America, I am certain that my folks and Colonel Daniel Boone's family went to Point Pleasant when I was five years old and Nathan Boone was seven years old, and so this would make it in 1787 when Colonel Daniel Boone and family first went to Point Pleasant.

Nathan Boone: I have shown you the family records, which in my father's own handwriting show his birth to have been October 22, 1734. This date is according to the old calendar, or Old Style, as he and my mother always expressed their disapproval of adopting the New Style calendar. Please note that this date also corresponds with the ideas of my cousins, Daniel Bryan and Mr. Lemon, who give the birthdays of their mothers, both sisters of my father. Mr. Lemon's mother, being next older than Colonel Boone, was born in February 1733, and Mr. Bryan's mother, next younger, was born in 1736.[2]

I would also add that my father heard that the old Quaker records in Pennsylvania recorded the date of his birth two years anterior to that which he had preserved, which always puzzled him. Yet he was not inclined to adopt this new date, which was July 14, 1732. Personally I feel that there must be some error in this date, and since it positively contradicts the other data given, I would not think of adopting it.

My father always said he was born in what was then Berks County, now Bucks County, Pennsylvania, fifty miles from Philadelphia. There my grandfather, Squire Boone, married Miss Sarah Morgan, a Quaker girl, who also lived in Bucks County about fifty miles from Philadelphia. This indicates he married within the Quaker Church and probably lived in the same neighborhood as my grandmother. I have often heard that my grandparents were early settlers in Berks County; in those times they could still catch shad in the Schuylkill River.

Draper: Both Reading, Oley, and Exeter are about fifty miles from Philadelphia.

Nathan Boone: I have often heard my father say his mother was a Morgan and related to General Daniel Morgan, hero of the Revolution. He spoke of General Morgan as his relative. He also said that his father was married in America and his mother was a woman of great neatness and industry in her housekeeping.

My grandfather, Squire Boone, was a weaver and farmer. His residence was probably in Oley. He kept at least five or six looms going at one time. He had his homestead and in the grass season moved his stock several miles distant to a fine range where cowpens were made for herding the cattle at nights, and a cabin was built in which Mrs. Boone spent the dairy season in attending to her milk. During the mild weather her son Daniel went with her to act as a herdsman. He went with the cattle during their daily roaming through the woods and brought them back each evening. This was his chief occupation from the age of ten to seventeen. This move was an annual affair, and Mrs. Boone always went personally to attend to the dairy, and her son Daniel was always her attendant to watch and take care of the cattle.

My father soon became fond of life in the woods. Even at the age of ten he would carry a club, a grub dug up by the roots, nicely shaven down, leaving a rooty knob at the end, which he called his herdsman's club. He became an expert in using it to kill birds and small game. This life enabled him to study their habits. When he was twelve or thirteen, his father bought him a gun, and he became a good marksman. The only problem was that he often neglected his herding duties to hunt, but this experience gave him his love of woods and hunting.

Daniel's brother Samuel was born in 1728 according to the records of Squire Boone Jr. Samuel had a very intelligent wife who taught my father to read, spell, and write a little. This was all the education Daniel ever had, as he never attended school. But he acquired more education by his own efforts, particularly in writing, as he could at first do little more than rudely write his own name.

I often heard my father, Colonel Daniel Boone, speak of the village of Oley and of Monocasy Creek and of Neversink Mountain. I think they were a dozen miles or more from the town of Reading, where his parents and relatives resided. My father remembered the small creek in the neighborhood when he was there in 1789 visiting Isaac Boone, James Boone, the schoolmaster, and some two or three other cousins.

His father, Squire Boone Sr., joined several of his neighbors in buying a seine, and in the spring of each year he would catch large quantities of shad in the Schuylkill not more than six or eight miles from his home. The partners would divide them and thus have enough salt from them for family use.

When my father was about seventeen the family left Pennsylvania and moved to North Carolina. It is likely that the Boone family left in the spring of 1751.

Draper: The land records show it was really in the spring of 1750 that Squire Boone Sr. sold his Berks County farm and moved away.

Nathan Boone: William L. Boone told me they tarried two years on Linville Creek in Virginia, and then in 1752 (perhaps summer or early fall) they moved to the Yadkin River valley, and that Elizabeth Boone, Colonel Daniel Boone's sister, got married the latter part of that year. Mrs. Lemon says it was in 1752 on the Yadkin.

I saw Henry Miller at his ironworks in Augusta County about 1790, when my father went as a representative of Mason County to the Virginia legislature. I was with my mother and father and spent the winter at Richmond while he was a member, and on his return we visited and spent some time with Miller in Augusta. Henry Miller had two sons, one now a merchant in New Franklin, Howard County, Missouri, nearly opposite Booneville, back from the river; and the other lives on the fork of the Lamine, some forty miles above the mouth of that fork and about that distance from Boonville, and near a place known as Blezo [Little Boone] Plains.

To the best of my knowledge, Henry Miller always lived in the Augusta region of Virginia and never in Pennsylvania, and the early friendship of Daniel Boone and Henry Miller was while the Boone family resided in Linville. My father's association with Miller goes far to convince me that the Boone family very likely resided for a time in Virginia. Grandfather Squire Boone Sr. owned a blacksmith's shop and employed Miller to work in it at blacksmithing and gunsmithing. My father, Daniel Boone, was placed in the shop to work with him and learn the trade from Miller. Miller was perhaps a year or two or three years older than my father and was full of fun and frolic.

There was a young man, George Wilcoxen, who wanted to go deer hunting and borrowed a long musket from Squire Boone. As he knew nothing of guns and shooting, Squire loaded the gun for him to use the next morning. That evening young Daniel and Henry Miller withdrew the ball and put in powder, balls, and shot enough for half a dozen charges. After Wilcoxen picked up the gun, the boys had misgivings for fear it would kill him. They heard a loud explosion and ran to meet Wilcoxen, and found his face covered with blood. His nose and face were badly bruised, and there was a gash in his forehead down to the skull. They said, "Why Wilcoxen, you have certainly killed a deer, as you have so much blood on you?" But he didn't know. They then went to look and found he had. Squire Boone knew the light load he had put in the gun wouldn't have done that damage. This same Wilcoxen was related to the Wilcoxen man who married Daniel Boone's oldest sister, Sarah.[3]

Some thirty [or more] odd years ago, while Daniel Boone was still living, an son of Henry Miller's older than the two already mentioned came to Missouri with his brother-in-law Moffet to look at land with the idea of coming west, perhaps starting an ironworks, as they had old Henry Miller's equipment, but never did.

I am very confident it was not in Pennsylvania that Henry Miller worked for Squire Boone Sr. It was either in Virginia or on the Yadkin River, but most probably in Virginia. When he was young my father, Daniel, helped his father with the farming but would go hunting at the slightest opportunity.

I remember the name Dutchman's Creek; my father was a part-time worker in teaming for his father. He would carry produce, furs, and peltry to market at Salisbury, North Carolina. The deer skins he took to market were generally half-dressed, that is the hair was taken off, and the grain (or outer thin skin in which the hair takes root) was scraped off and dried. This left the skin soft, which meant they could be packed more snugly. His work as a teamster was mostly in the summer season; thus he would spend most of his time in falls and winters in hunting. He hunted not only because he was fond of that roving life but because it was profitable. Deer skins and furs were very valuable in that period. Until this age my father had only hunted occasionally for pleasure and recreation, but now he began to do it for profit and as a business of life.

In 1755 my father, Daniel Boone, was on Braddock's campaign during the French and Indian War. He was not a soldier but served as a teamster conveying the baggage of the army. When General Braddock's army was defeated near Pittsburgh, he was with the baggage in the rear of the column. When the retreat began he cut his team loose from the wagon and escaped with his horses. He used to censure Braddock's conduct, saying he neglected to keep out spies and flank guards. I think that somehow my father was connected with Washington's colonial troops; he often spoke of Washington, whom both he and my mother personally knew.[4]

Draper: Perhaps your father met General George Washington when the Boone and the Bryan families resided in the Valley of Virginia.

Nathan Boone: This is possible, but it is more likely they met at Fredericksburg in 1762.

I do not recall that Father performed any other service during the French and Indian War. I don't think he was on Montgomery's or Grant's Cherokee campaigns, but sometimes he talked about Colonel Byrd's campaign and his dilatoriness and failure. However, these opinions may have been from some other source, perhaps the Van Bibbers.[5]

Olive Boone: I often heard Colonel Daniel Boone speak of Byrd's expedition in 1761. He always criticized Byrd for his slowness and failure, but I can't recall whether Colonel Boone actually said he was on this expedition. But Nathan and I both feel that his father would not have spoken that way about Colonel Byrd, had he not have been an eyewitness.

Draper: Mr. Haywood says that immediately after the peace of 1761, Daniel Boone and others went hunting in the Holston Valley and East Tennessee, which leads me to think that he was on the campaign with Colonel Byrd.[6] Daniel Boone probably served as one of Colonel Waddell's men and, after being discharged from the army camp on Holston, went hunting on the way home.

Nathan Boone: I have often heard my father and mother speak of Fort Dobbs but have no recollection as to whether they forted there or not.[7] Frankly, I do not believe that our family was forced to live in a fort after they settled on the Yadkin River, nor can I recall anything further about the French War. Of course, it was while out with Braddock that my father met Finley, who told him about Kentucky. For some time I was in doubt who first told Father about the place, but I have now decided it was Finley.[8]

Draper: In December 1759, a peace treaty was made with the Cherokees, but there was no peace, as the Indians attacked Fort Prince George in January 1760. It is well known that some traders who returned to the Indian towns were killed. In the midst of all this, your father, Daniel Boone, appears to have been hunting on the Watauga River, as he carved "D Boone 1760" on a tree. Did he ever speak of this?

Nathan Boone: Even when the Indians were at war with us, Father and the other hunters would still go out but would avoid the Indian paths and thoroughfares. Obviously he ventured over the mountains into East Tennessee. I have often heard Father speak of hunting in the Smoky, Brushy, and Little Mountains, and also Pilot Mountain. While hunting in and passing over these mountains, he would never consider he had discovered the real West, which was Kentucky. The real West was the land beyond the Cumberland and Pine mountain chain. The first party to venture beyond these mountains was led by the explorer Dr. Walker in 1760. I do not doubt that my father moved from the South Fork of the Yadkin River farther west to the head of Yadkin Valley, but this was before I was born, so I can tell you nothing about it.

Of course it is well known that my father traveled all the way to Florida. As he became acquainted with the Slaughters and Fields, he must first have been in Culpepper County, Virginia; otherwise they would not have joined him on the Florida trip. I would suppose the trip was made about 1768.

The party that went to Florida consisted of William Hill, a man named Slaughter, and one named Field. I do not remember who else was in the group. They started from home near the close of summer to explore the Florida country. They traveled to Pensacola and explored a few days up the St. John's River, but they didn't like the country. They found that the palmetto trees had large leaves which thickly skirted the streams. For a few hundred yards from the streams the ground was good for planting, but farther from the creeks it became dry and elevated; most of the soil turned into sand and was worthless. On the whole, my father was not satisfied with the country, yet he purchased a house lot and would have moved to it, had not my mother been unwilling to go so far from her connections and friends.

Slaughter was fond of gambling and won money going and coming back from Florida. This, along with the deer skins of the party, was enough to meet most of their expenses while passing through the settlements. In Florida the only game they found when hunting was deer and some birds.

Mr. Hill was a fellow who was full of mischief, and whenever they would stop, he would demonstrate this trait. He had a way of snapping sticks at the girls between his thumb and finger. I heard a story about a girl Hill had been teasing who turned his saddled and bridled horse loose while he was eating. While he went after it, she heated the blade of his knife. When he returned and tried to cut butter with it, the butter slid away. The girl said, "Mr. Hill, your knife is ashamed of the butter." Hill, discovering the trick, took out his pocketknife, saying he had a knife that was never ashamed to cut butter.

At another time, eating out of a very dirty wooden noggin, Hill said that was a lucky noggin, in that it had escaped many a hard scouring.

My father had agreed to be at home to eat his Christmas dinner with mother and his family. He said he could have got home a few days sooner but delayed his trip so that at noon on Christmas he walked in and took his seat at dinner at home. He told me the fort at Pensacola was on a point of land projecting into the water. I have no knowledge of what became of Hill and Slaughter.

During an early fall hunt, before my father went to Kentucky, he and others were camped in the Watauga region and saw an unusually large bear. This bear was very poor and unfit for use. It crossed a deep gully on a fallen tree within some twenty yards from camp, made a circuit down the stream running southerly, and then in a short distance it ran off in a westerly direction. This bear had an unusual white strip on the nose. Father always said many bears had yellow spots but rarely white ones. He said he had killed many a bear and never saw more than one or two with white spots on the nose; but many had a large white spot on the breast. In any event, the size and marks of this bear were unusual.

About the close of December, while still at the same camp, my father and his companions saw the very same bear, as they fully believed, returning by the very route he went and crossing the same fallen tree, traveling eastwardly, now well fattened. One of the party shot and killed him. That year there was no mast [food] such as bear were known to fatten on, except in the western part of the Cherokee territory. This bear food could only be found in the great bear masting region of Tombigbee and Bear Creek, and Father then concluded that this bear by some instinct must have traveled that great distance for food to get fat and then returned to its old haunt to take up its winter den and sleep. He told me that unless they are fat, they will not den up for winter but will ramble about, eating whatever they can find. My father, Daniel Boone, used to say that when he was out on fall bear hunts, he would watch and see in what general direction the bear would go, then traveling that way, he would be sure to find plenty of bears in some plenteous masting region.

Draper: Mr. Haywood said that Colonel Daniel Boone was on the Rockcastle River in Kentucky in 1764 and there met the long hunters Blevins, Wallen, and Skaggs.[9] He also said that on this trip he was exploring Kentucky for Henderson and Company. Do you know about such a trip?

Nathan Boone: I have no recollection of any trip Father made to Kentucky at that time, nor his meeting with those long hunters, nor exploring the country for Henderson. Frankly, I would discount such a tale, as I am pretty certain he never was employed by Henderson's company until 1774 or 1775. My father used to speak of his trip to Sandy as his first attempt to find Kentucky and said that it was a failure.

In the fall of about 1767, my father and probably his brother, Squire Boone, and William Hill started from Yadkin River in search of the Kentucky country. This was the place that Finley had told him about in 1755. Hill was the same man who went on the Florida trip; I think he was also from Yadkin country. My father had great confidence in him, a matter of great consequence to the early hunters. When your partner and you separated to hunt, you had to be certain of meeting again at the hunting camp at the specified time. William Hill was frequently with my father on hunting trips; and they made an agreement that whoever should die first would return and give the other information about the spirit world. Hill died first, but Father used to say he never received the promised intelligence from the spirit land. I would suppose he died not long after this trip to the Big Sandy River, as I heard no more of him. I would assume if he had been living, he would probably have been on the Kentucky hunt in 1769-1771, as he and Father were such great cronies.

In 1767 they crossed the mountains with the intention of reaching the Ohio River. They came to the headwaters of the Big Sandy, and

Two views of Nathan Boone's stone house in St. Charles County, Missouri.

from its course they decided that it must flow into the Ohio. So they continued down it, but after traveling about a hundred miles, they were caught in a severe snowstorm and were forced to remain in camp there all winter. This camp was near what was later known as Young's salt-works, on the eastern bank of the Sandy River. I think this camp was about a hundred miles from the Ohio. The country around the Big Sandy River was forbidding, hilly with much laurel, and my father and the others became discouraged. When spring came, they returned home to North Carolina. Oddly enough, afterwards my father didn't know the name of the stream upon which he wintered.

William Hill was a man after my father's own heart. He was fond of the wilderness, hunting, and wild adventure—a jolly good companion for such a lonely life. In the winter of 1796-1797 my father and I spent the winter in that region hunting; it was then when Father told me of this trip. It was near this camp where I saw my first buffaloes at a salt springs there.

Olive Boone: I heard Colonel Daniel Boone and his wife say that the first time they ever saw each other was at a wedding.

Draper: Probably when William Bryan and Mary Boone were married in 1753.

Olive Boone: I suppose, and if there was any "shining of eyes," it must have been there.[10] The second time they met was at some place where several young people met to eat cherries. They sat upon a ridge of green turf under the cherry trees, and Daniel Boone was beside Rebecca Bryan and doubtless turning over in his own mind whether she would make him a good companion. At that time he took out his knife and, taking up one corner of her white apron, began to cut and stab holes through it, to which she said nothing nor offered any resistance. Daniel Boone afterward used to say he did it to try her temper, thinking if it was fiery, she would fly into a passion. When they were married, two other couples were married at the same time.

Draper: Boone was sometimes odd enough to ordinary appearance; but as in this case, he had a purpose in his singular ways.

Nathan Boone: After he was married, Father lived for a while in a house in my grandfather's yard and then settled on a place of his own. He would farm it sufficiently for family purposes, but he would depend upon hunting during the fall and winter for cash. With this money he would purchase such articles as the family needed which they could not produce. Oftentimes he would haul goods in his wagon for hire. His hunts would generally extend for two or three months, and sometimes on his shorter trips, he would take his oldest son, James, out with him. He began taking James on hunts when he was seven or eight years old; and sometimes during a cold, snowy spell, Father would have difficulty in keeping little James comfortably warm and could do so only by hugging him up to him.

Olive Boone: I have heard Colonel Daniel Boone say that when a very small boy, smallpox infected the neighborhood, so his mother kept all the children closely confined at home to prevent their catching it. But Daniel and his elder sister Elizabeth became weary of this confinement and decided their only hope to get out of the house was to catch the smallpox. They reasoned that when they recovered, they would again be free to go where they pleased in the neighborhood. So one night they got up from their beds, stole off, and went to a neighbor's where they had the smallpox. Here they proceeded to go into the sick person's room, lay down beside the patient, and then returned home. Soon they began to be sick, and their old Quaker mother, suspecting the smallpox, called Daniel and said, "Now Daniel, I want thee to tell me the truth." So Daniel confessed fully, and she said "Thee nasty stinking gorrels—why did thee not tell me, so that I could have had thee better prepared?" They got through it, as did the other children, very easily.

Another time there was a mischievous youth in the neighborhood who got Daniel and a friend into a fistfight with each other, in which Daniel had a front tooth loosed. (It remained loose until a year or so before his death, when one of his daughters pulled it with her fingers.) The two boys realized the trick that had been played on them and in turn caught the meddler and gave him a severe chastisement.

The family also tells a story of Daniel when he was still quite young. His father, Squire Boone, caught a large quantity of fish at the river, and his mother proceeded to clean all she wanted. Afterwards there were fish left, so she sent word to a poor woman to go and get the remainder.

After Mrs. Boone went home, Daniel lay down on a dry flat rock, placed his hat over his face, intending to take a nap. Soon after, the woman's two daughters came for the fish and, seeing a pail of entrails from the fish Mrs. Boone had cleaned, took up the pail and emptied the whole in Daniel's face. He thought if they were fond of such rough joking he would pay them back in a rough way and gave them a good beating, sending them off with bloody noses. Their mother went to Mrs. Boone to complain, but she said, "If thee has not brought up thy daughters to better behavior, it was high time they were taught good manners. They had got no more than they deserved."[11]

2

THE HUNTER

Nathan Boone: When [John] Finley came to North Carolina in 1768 or 1769, he looked up my father, Daniel Boone, whom he had not seen since the Braddock campaign. I have no recollection about Finley's appearance, character, size, or age. But while he was there my father told him how he had attempted to reach Kentucky by way of the Big Sandy River and had failed. Finley said there must be a better way across the mountains than along the Big Sandy River; the Cherokee Indians frequently went to war against the northern Indians and must have a path across the mountains. Eventually Finley and my father made an agreement to raise a few men and attempt to penetrate through the mountains farther to the westwards, using the Indian warpath. Finley, who was an Indian trader, could describe the Ohio River but did not seem to know anything about the interior of the country.

Lyman Draper: I would suppose the reason for this is that he had only traveled from the Big Bone Lick to Lulbegrud Creek and back along the same route. He had never been on the eminence between Rockcastle and the Kentucky River or over the Cumberland Mountains.

Nathan Boone: The particular times about this trip and the details of Squire Boone's arrival or when Finley, [James] Mooney, and the others went back, I cannot remember. But both Olive and I well remember that my father, Daniel Boone, used to speak of being captured three times, although one of the times could scarcely be called a captivity. But I can no longer remember how or when that occurred. I do remember that Alexander Neeley was the man who came out to Kentucky with

Squire Boone, but which time I don't remember. I suppose my father's narrative published by Filson and Daniel Bryan's statement would have the best information.[1]

In that case my father, Daniel Boone, and John Stewart were in Kentucky in December, reconnoitering or hunting, when several Indians rushed out and made them show them to the their hunting camp. This they were willing to do. They hoped they could sacrifice the skins at the first camp and save the rest. They probably found one of the party there taking care of it, and Father or Stewart gave him orders to leave slyly and give notice to the others at the remaining camps and have the furs, horses, peltry, and other valuables hid. But when Father and Stewart reached them in turn, to their mortification and disappointment they found nothing removed, and all the skins and provisions fell into the hands of the Indians except for the guns and some ammunition for the men out hunting. When the Indians left, they give a parting warning about wasps and yellow jackets stinging them if they should ever return to Kentucky again.

Draper: I would think that the Indians gave your father and Stewart this warning when they were captured the second time, trying to steal the Indian's horses. They were not too hostile if they permitted these hunters to retain their guns and a supply of ammunition sufficient to kill game on their return home, but maybe they would tell them not to return again to Kentucky to kill the beavers and other game.

Nathan Boone: I do know that they were plundered and unsupplied for a winter's hunt. It was then my father thought best to make an effort to recover some of the horses from the Indians so as to be able either to return home altogether, or else for someone of the party to go and get a supply of ammunition and other necessaries. With some such views, after the Indians were thought to have got beyond the distance to pursue, Father and Stewart started out and instructed the others to wait and see if they could recapture the horses. After two days they overtook the Indians, who were camped with their horses wandering around and some of them belled. Putting bells on a few has a tendency to keep them together. I still put bells on one or more in the field for that very purpose.

That night my father and Stewart took four or five of the horses and rode for the remainder of that night. During all the following day and night, they kept up their flight but stopped a few minutes the next morning about sunrise on the sunny side of a hill to warm themselves by the rays of the sun. Stewart was in the act of tying his moccasin when my father put his ear on the ground and thought he heard something like a roaring noise. He raised his head and looked back to see the glittering of the rising sun on the Indians' guns just as the war party came over the brow of the hill towards them. The Indian party was on horseback and too near for my father and Stewart to attempt an escape.

The Indians came up with cheerful countenances and no signs of anger, but whooping and laughing, as though they were making sport of my father and Stewart as not being smart enough to evade them. They took one of the bells from a horse, fastened it around my father's neck, and made him run around and jingle it. In broken English they delighted in saying, "Steal horse, ha?"

Draper: Did your father say that during the night he was confined between Indians and perhaps fastened, or that a cord was stretched over the prisoners and the Indians on each side of them while they were sleeping, so the Indians could feel any movement made by their prisoners?

Olive Boone: No, but the leader of the Indians was Captain Will.

Draper: I would suppose he was the Shawnee who resided at and gave the name to Willstown on the Miami River.

Nathan Boone: These Indians were Shawnees. Later Captain Will was with the Shawnees who captured my father and the salt boilers in 1778.

The Indians were steering their course for the Ohio, as they lived not far beyond it. The Indians kept promising to release my father and Stewart; however, they kept them prisoner for seven days. It was not until they were within a day's journey of the Ohio that they got away. That was a good thing, because my father had resolved he would not cross this river.

On the evening of the seventh day, at dusk while the Indians were busy making camp, my father and Stewart, on an agreed signal, each snatched a gun and some ammunition and dodged into the thick cane at the edge of the camp. The Indians could not find them before dark, and after dark they stopped trying. Boone and Stewart quietly made their escape. Both Olive and I have often heard my father tell this story.

I should mention that, as most of the Shawnee were then residing on the Miami, this party was probably traveling on the old Indian trail leading to the crossing near the mouth of Licking River or perhaps on the more easterly trail crossing about four miles above the mouth of Little Sandy River near Hanging Rock.[2]

When my father and John Stewart finally returned to Station Camp, they found everyone gone. Although I don't remember Father mentioning this, I would presume that he and Stewart took the trail of their companions and overtook them on Rockcastle River, about thirty-five or forty miles from camp. At that time he was overjoyed to find his brother Squire, who had come out to Kentucky, probably with Neeley. I believe my Uncle Squire had accidentally found the Station Camp but, when hearing that my father and Stewart had gone to recover their horses but had not returned, concluded they were either killed or captured. Then they all left Station Camp for home.

Draper: Squire Boone and Neeley had brought out new supplies, probably horses as well as traps and ammunition, so the Boones decided to remain and have a winter hunt. We know that the others, discouraged, returned home. Do you know what ever happened to Finley?

Nathan Boone: I know nothing more about [John] Finley, [Joseph] Holden, or [William] Cooley, but my father said that in 1774 Mooney was a spy on the campaign and in the battle of Point Pleasant, maybe in Shelby's company, and was killed in the battle. I would agree that he was a spy, but I think he was probably killed before the battle.

Draper: You're right about that, and I have documents to prove it. I also remember that your father said in his narrative that one man came out with Squire Boone in the first instance and subsequently returned home by himself. Daniel Bryan says the same but doesn't remember who he was or much about it; but he mentions that when Squire Boone came out the second time (May 1, 1770, according to Daniel Bryan, or July 1770, according to Daniel Boone's narrative by Filson), Alexander Neeley and Jesse Boone came with him.[3]

Nathan Boone: Both Olive and I remember the name Neeley but

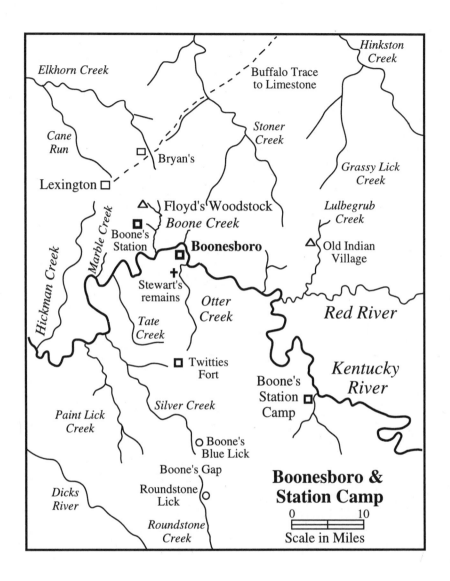

Elkhorn Creek

Hinkston
Creek

Buffalo Trace
to Limestone

Cane
Run

Stoner
Creek

Bryan's

Grassy Lick
Creek

Lexington

Floyd's Woodstock

Lulbegrub
Creek

Boone Creek

Boone's
Station

Boonesboro

Old Indian
Village

Marble Creek

Stewart's
remains

Hickman Creek

*Otter
Creek*

Red River

*Tate
Creek*

Twitties
Fort

**Kentucky
River**

Boone's
Station
Camp

Paint Lick
Creek

Silver Creek

Boone's
Blue Lick

Boone's Gap

**Boonesboro &
Station Camp**

*Dicks
River*

Roundstone
Lick

0   10

*Roundstone
Creek*

Scale in Miles

have no recollection whatever about Jesse Boone going to Kentucky. Jesse's father, Israel, brother of my father, Daniel Boone, died of consumption at an early age. His wife had previously died, and as no other Boones ever had it, it was thought he caught it from his wife. Young Jesse was raised by my father and mother. Jesse was always unlucky, first breaking his leg and then his arm. We don't believe that Jesse Boone came to Kentucky during this hunt; Neeley was the man who came out with Squire Boone and returned home by himself.[4]

Draper: Daniel Bryan says that Neeley came out with Squire Boone in December 1769 but soon returned; and finally that Squire Boone started back after supplies in order to rejoin his brother and Stewart the first day of May ensuing. On the other hand, Colonel Daniel Boone says in his narrative that Squire Boone didn't start back for supplies until May 1, 1770, and that he returned the following July 27 according to agreement. I am at present most inclined to believe this version of Colonel Daniel Boone's.

Nathan Boone: I agree with you. Incidentally, I am sorry that I wrote you that I had forgotten why my father and Stewart had separated prior to Stewart disappearing.

Olive Boone: I distinctly remember that Colonel Daniel Boone and Stewart had only separated to hunt or trap for some designated period and were then to meet at camp. Nathan and I now agree on this point. We clearly remember hearing Daniel Boone tell us that their camp was on or near the northern bank of the Kentucky River, not the old Station Camp, but lower down the river and not far from the mouth of the Red River. He said Stewart went to the south side of the Kentucky River and he to the north side, or at least the sequel would seem to indicate it. After they separated, there was very wet weather for midwinter, and the Kentucky River became flooded and overflowed its banks.

Nathan Boone: Father was very emphatic in pointing out the incident did not occur at the old Station Camp.[5] He said that he reached the camp at the appointed time, and he attributed Stewart's absence to the swollen state of the river. After a few days when the waters fell, my father crossed the river nearly opposite his camp. He went to the nearest high land to the backing waters, and there found the remains of a recent fire, which had apparently been used a couple of days, with the initials of Stewart's name freshly cut in the bark of a nearby tree. No other clue or evidence of him could be found. Until Stewart's remains were found in 1775, many surmised that he had taken that occasion to run off and abandon his friends and family; but both my parents used to say that he was a man of warm feelings and devoted to his family and never had any difficulty with his wife. My father even said he never had a brother he thought more of than he did of John Stewart. He had all the confidence in him that one man could have in another; he was faithful in the performance of his promises, a most essential requisite, as Father always said, in a hunting companion. Those who went to Kentucky had a strong feeling that only some unusual misfortune could cause him to disappear. My father always thought that Stewart either got killed or sickened and died in the wilderness.

As you may have heard, this mystery was not solved until spring 1775. At that time my father was with a party making the road from Powell Valley to the Kentucky River at the Big Lick, where Boonesborough was afterward located. Not far from the end of the route, after taking up camp, a member of the group discovered human bones in a hollow tree. They also found a powder horn which belonged to John Stewart; my father would have recognized it even if his name had not been found plainly engraved upon it. To put your name on a powder horn was a universal practice with all the early frontiersmen.

Father also said he thought he could recognize Stewart's well-known features from his skull. They discovered that one of his arms had been broken and found the discoloration of the lead ball still distinctly discernible on the bone. There was no other injury to be seen. Stewart's rifle could not be found. My father always felt that Stewart had cut the initials on the tree, either for amusement or to show he had been there, while the water was high and then was attacked there (or perhaps at a camp on higher ground). He was shot and dropped his rifle while making his escape, either from haste or because of his wounded arm.

John Stewart was married to my father's youngest sister, Hannah, and according to Daniel Bryan, he left four children. His widow often preached in public on the Quaker faith. She subsequently married a man with the name of Pennington and settled down in the Green River country of Kentucky. We know nothing of her descendants either by John Stewart or Mr. Pennington.[6]

Draper: As Boone and Stewart had been captured by Indians on December 22, 1769, then showed their campsites, retook their horses, and were themselves recaptured, kept seven days by the Indians, then returned to their old Station Camp, making about thirteen or fourteen days, it would be approximately January 4, 1770, when they reached their Station Camp, from which the others must have departed the day before. Since [Daniel] Boone and Stewart overtook them thirty-five or forty miles off at Rockcastle River, with Boone, Stewart, and Neeley returning, it must have been pretty well along in January or early February when Stewart was killed.

Where Squire Boone was when Daniel Boone and John Stewart parted is unknown. But it is plain from the Daniel Boone narrative by Filson that it was after the loss of Stewart that Neeley started home by himself; and Daniel and Squire Boone made a shelter and kept together so that they might not get separated and lost. Squire Boone started for home with the furs of the winter's hunt, which must have been almost entirely beaver and probably some of the less plentiful otter. He was robbed by the way, as Moses and Isaiah Boone say and as was noted by Isaac Shelby.

Nathan Boone: I don't know about that. It may be that Squire Boone was robbed on his return home in the fall of 1770, when the streams would be swollen as represented. By the time Uncle Squire left Kentucky in May 1770, they had hunted so industriously that the supply of ammunition was almost exhausted. For this reason my father was obliged to conserve what he had left to supply himself with game for food. Thus he had to forgo the pleasure of a summer deer hunt. After the Indian robbery and the departure of Finley, Holden, Cooley, and Mooney, my father and his remaining companions didn't occupy the old Station Camp but made new camps as new hunting localities required.

My father seldom stayed two nights at one place after Stewart's disappearance. When Uncle Squire left, my father decided to explore the country. He discovered several of the noted salt licks or springs, which in every case were easily found by following the well-beaten buffalo roads leading to them. He visited the Upper and Lower Blue Licks on the

In 1837, Nathan Boone sold his home in St. Charles County, Missouri, paid off some debts, and built this "dog trot" cabin in southwest Missouri on the headwaters of the Osage River. Courtesy of Missouri Dept. of Natural Resources.

Licking River. At the latter place he saw thousands of buffaloes, with other animals resorting there to lick the ground and drink the water. He kept on down Licking River a few miles below the lick to where the old Indian warpath crossed, then went along a trail to the Ohio, which he reached about twenty-five miles above the mouth of Licking River. He then followed the southern shore of the Ohio River down to the Falls of Ohio. When passing the Big Bone Lick he saw Indians. There were also two or three instances when he saw Indians on the northern shore of the Ohio, all of whom he avoided without being discovered. Near the lower end of the Falls of Ohio, on the Kentucky shore, he found the remains of what was an old trading house.[7] There he found part of a chimney, about four feet high, made of stone. There was also some of the picketing, made of split logs inserted endwise in the ground, that still remained.

The place had apparently been occupied about twelve or fifteen years before he arrived.

He then went across country to an old hunting region, during which time he again struck and passed the Kentucky River, very likely near the present Frankfort. There he saw an Indian fishing, sitting upon that part of a fallen tree projecting over the water, and he afterward simply said, "While I was looking at him he tumbled into the river and I saw no more of him." It was understood from the way in which he spoke of it that he had shot and killed the Indian; yet he seemed not to care about alluding more particularly to it.

Draper: When you remember the Indians had robbed him and his companions of all their peltry, furs, horses, and other valuables and had twice captured him and Stewart and finally killed Stewart, one can no doubt conclude he thought this fellow was just one of a war party camped nearby, ready to do him harm. Under the circumstances, he would have been wise to end his life. Afterwards, according to the Filson narrative, Daniel met his brother, Squire Boone, who returned to their old camp on July 27.

Nathan Boone: Daniel Bryan contends that Squire Boone returned again to North Carolina for supplies, traps, and for their coming winter's hunt, which I suppose is true.[8]

Olive Boone: Certainly Squire Boone made a second return trip in the fall. This goes to confirm the idea of Squire Boone's returning in the fall and getting robbed, and the Indians getting drowned by high autumnal waters. This robbery delayed him in his return. I think that if Squire stayed beyond the allotted period, Daniel would have been uneasy and would have started to meet his brother. If he failed to find him, he would have gone on home rather than remain alone in Kentucky during the winter. He would not have lingered in Kentucky had he been uncertain as to his brother's fate.

I have heard that when Daniel was waiting for Squire, he met an aged Indian who had been left to die by his tribe. He then killed a deer and, keeping only a small quantity, gave the rest to the old Indian. Afterward he continued on, discovered a large, dry tree on fire, and there found Squire.

Nathan Boone: By the time Squire arrived in Kentucky, it was probably December, as there was some snow on the ground. They soon after went to the Green River country, and according to Father, there they met a party of long hunters. He said he was out hunting and returned to their camp one evening, and two of the camp tenders had a bloody fistfight caused by a dispute respecting the natural history of the wood tick, a pestilent little insect common in the western wilderness.

The summer and fall hunt must have yielded entirely deer skins, and these only half-dressed. Graining means (if the hair doesn't get rubbed off) the scraping off of the hair and the grain, like a cussier leather; then when dry the leather is rubbed across a staking board until it becomes somewhat soft; then it is said to be half-dressed and fit for compact packing. A heavily packed horse could carry about a hundred half-dressed deer skins of two pounds each.

The beaver skins were stretched within hoops, generally of grapevine, and dried. First the skin is ripped from the underjaw down in the skinning. The otter skin is taken off cased, that is, ripped off whole; a bow or drying board is run into the skin after it has been turned inside out. A horse can pack nearly two hundred beaver or otter skins, as each weighs about 1¼ pounds. This is the average weight of beaver skins, and one pound for otters. In those days deer skins were probably worth about forty cents a pound or a dollar each, while beaver skins were then worth about two dollars and a half apiece and otter skins from three dollars to five dollars apiece. Preparing these skins was done in bad weather, when the men could not hunt, or evenings.

About 200 to 250 pounds of furs or peltry was considered the maximum load for a horse. Father and I, during a winter in Missouri, would catch 400 or 500 beaver and not more than 20 otter; so from 200 to 250 beaver skins was about the full amount of a successful winter's trapping. In Missouri beaver were more plentiful than they were in Kentucky. My father and another man once caught 900 pounds in a season. From 200 to 250 pounds would be a reasonable number for a hunter in Kentucky. Also 400 or 500 deer skins would be considered a fair season's hunt.

My father would sometimes hunt all day for deer. He would not just watch salt licks. He would start early in the morning, when the leaves were moistened with dew and thus caused no noise when walking, and deer generally were feeding. They are always on their feet feeding or walking about during the rising of the moon, to which hunters pay great respect. Deer are easier seen when on their feet and moving about than when lying down, and though there were particular hours in the day when they mostly fed, the hunters would keep hunting all day.

My father, Daniel Boone, practiced fire-hunting on the Yadkin River in North Carolina, but only in the summers. At that time the deer would come to the river to avoid the flies. There is also a tender moss in the shoaly parts of the river, which the deer sought after, and they would go there also to drink. As the banks of the rivers were often skirted with thick cane, it was more convenient to fire-hunt with canoes, though sometimes the hunters would wade in shallow streams and carry their fire. My father never fire-hunted in Kentucky or Missouri.

When trapping beaver the traps are set promiscuously in streams of some three or four inches of water and within half a dozen feet from shore. They are always put where the bank breaks off abruptly and makes deep water, at least three or four feet deep. A chain is attached to the trap, which if not long enough is lengthened by a cord, together making twelve or fifteen feet, and the other end fastened to a stake on shore.

The bait is beaver musk or castor, which has a rather pleasant odor, and this is rubbed on the upper end of a stick, the lower end of which is inserted in the ground at the edge of the water directly opposite to the trap, and sometimes a bush or two are stuck on each side of the trap so that when the swimming beaver come along and scent the musk, they will swim in to shore to smell it. They always swim with the forepaws placed upon the jaws and put them down whenever their breast touches anything. Their hind foot is broad-webbed for swimming—a good paddle. They put down their forepaws and thus touching the trap when smelling of the musk bait are caught; they then generally make out into deep water to get clear of the trap, and the weight of the trap will sink and drown them. Sometimes, however, when in deep water and failing thus to get clear of the encumbrance, the beaver will return again to shore and sometimes wring its caught paw (the bone of which is generally broken) in the trap till the skin is cut off, and then escape. The dismembered leg would soon heal, and hunters frequently catch them afterwards, sometimes even within a day or two of the loss of their foot. When they wring off a foot and escape, they generally hasten off several miles up or down the stream and are then as likely as any others to get entrapped again.

The otter is a more rambling, migratory creature than the beaver and hence is less frequently caught. The trap is set in the same manner as for beaver except for the bait. In fact, no bait at all is generally used or, if any, a fish or mussel is placed on a stick in front of the trap. Otter have particular places along a stream where they go on shore, either to roll or play or to go to some nearby pond, and these places are often points of sand or dirt at the mouth of some gully or ravine. Thus they make beaten paths, called in hunters' parlance "otter-slides," and where these start from the stream is where the trap is set. Their hide is tougher than the beaver, and they very seldom wring off their feet in the trap.

The hunters generally would place their half-dressed deer skins, beaver, and otter upon poles several feet from the ground, and pile several skins on top of each other and put a pole on top of them to keep them in their place. There would also be a pole on each side, swung across by cords, to keep the skins close together. The hanging skins were long enough to form a pack, nicely folded and fastened. A horse load is two packs, one swung on either side. The packs would also be placed on poles or scaffolds to be out of the reach of wolves, hungry bears, and other animals. Over both the skins on poles and the packs on scaffolds were placed deer or elk skins or bark to protect them from the weather.

The bear does not seem to lose flesh during his hibernation. It comes out in the spring and eats young nettles and other tender weeds, but seldom any grass, which makes them very poor. During the summer they eat very little of anything, only worms and bugs which they paw up on the ground and scratch from rotten logs. During this period, if they come across the skins of a hunter, they will tear them down, if within reach, then eat and destroy them. Wolves will eat and tear them up at any time. In the summer when berries appear, the bears eat them, along with wild fruits, and in the fall they feed on mast, acorns, hazelnuts, chestnuts, hickory nuts, and beechnuts. It is then that they gain fat very rapidly, and all their meat being thus so quickly acquired is what makes wild bear meat so sweet and tender. This is the opposite of tamed bear meat, where the animal is always kept well fed. The long hunters found bear skins were too heavy to carry to Carolina and were probably not marketable at that day.

My father once told me the story of Green's bear fight. This fellow Green, whom he knew, was out hunting with his brother-in-law about 1773. Green was at camp alone one day when a large bear came along. Green shot and wounded the bear but did not kill it. The bear attacked him, tore him badly, destroyed one eye, and gnawed on him for "as long as he wished." When Green's companions found him, they thought he could not live and abandoned him. When they returned to the settlements they reported his death. Green had no fire all winter; he dug a hole in the ground in the camp and put in a quantity of wild turkey feathers that he had saved prior to the accident. There was some bear meat hanging up in camp, which he ate sparingly. In the spring some men started from the settlement to bury him and met him on his way in. He was greatly disfigured but lived many years.[9]

The elk was not hunted for his hide. The hides were nearly valueless at market, and moreover, being from four to six times the weight of deer skins, they were too cumbersome to pack. The hunters would occasionally kill them, mainly to make tugs and straps of their hides. The meat was considered as good as venison, and hunters used it for variety or when buffalo, deer, or bear could not be obtained.

Otter were never eaten, but beaver were eaten, even though they were not very good. Beaver was mostly eaten when hunters were busily engaged trapping and did not wish to make a noise by shooting other game. The beaver tails were very oily and are much loved by some, but neither Father nor I esteemed them as a delicacy, though I will say that the tail was preferable to any other portion of the body. A beaver tail weighed from one to two pounds. During the winter months buffalo, elk, and deer were generally poor, and the fat bears had hibernated and were seldom found; at that time the beaver meat became a necessity.

The hunters, including my father when in Kentucky, would wear moccasins of deer skins, stuffed well with deer's hair to answer the place of stockings. These were very warm. Deerskin leggings were fastened at the top to a body belt on which the scabbard would also be attached. The leggings were then tied around below the knee. In the evening if the leggings and moccasins were wet, they were well dried and rubbed soft. The moccasins were taken off for the night, as they preserved far longer; the perspiration of the feet eventually destroyed the moccasin.

Hunters kept their feet to the fire at night, which would render the moccasin unnecessary. They never wore them nights unless apprehensive of danger, in which case they would then often tie them to their guns, ready to be snatched up at a moment. This lying with the feet to the fire is what the old hunters attributed their uniform good health to. The only other garment made of deer skins was the outer garment or hunting shirt. My father, Daniel Boone, always despised the raccoon fur caps and did not wear one himself, as he always had a hat.

After leaving the long hunters and the Green River country, my father and Uncle Squire returned home. With the proceeds of their winter's hunt, they intended to pay their debts, including those that Squire Boone contracted in the fall of 1770 when he had been robbed. Unfortunately, on the way they were robbed of all they had by a party of Cherokees and forced to flee for their lives. So my father's circumstances were not improved by his long hunt, due to the robberies by the Indians as previously mentioned. My father also lost some packs stolen from his camps during his absence while hunting and trapping. I do not remember the particulars of this Cherokee robbery.

During the long Kentucky hunt and exploration, my father had no dog with him. He did not often take dogs, except when bear hunting in North Carolina. When he lived on Yadkin and hunted over to Watauga or went into Brushy Mountain, he often traveled with John Robertson. Robertson would always take some well-trained bear dogs with him. When near home, he would pack in some of the bear skins.

Olive Boone: About 1762 there was a Mr. Tate, an old hunter, much from home, who resided on Yadkin near our family and the Bryans. Once Colonel Boone came home from hunting and threshing out rye at his father-in-law's farm for himself, and hearing of Tate's family being destitute because of Tate's long absence hunting, he asked Mr. Bryan if he could also thresh out and give Tate's family a small supply. He agreed, and when Boone, on the way home, passed the Tate's house, he gave some grain to Mrs. Tate. When her husband returned, he became jealous of Boone without cause and spoke of it. Later Boone met with him, gave him a severe flogging, and said he would do it again if he ever threw out any similar intimations. Boone said he would be grateful if under similar circumstances anyone would be kind enough to befriend his family as he had attempted to befriend Tate's. He insisted he would not let his kindness be misconstrued in that ungrateful manner.[10]

Draper: Do you remember the story of the wolf robbing Daniel Boone's cave camp, a tale told by the late Boone Hays, or a mission with Robertson from the Watauga country to the Cherokees in 1772? Haywood says that Daniel Boone moved to East Tennessee about 1769 and that he was on the Watauga in 1772.[11]

Nathan Boone: No, I do not recall any such stories, but I feel confident my father and his family lived a while on the Watauga, for it was there where Jemima Boone got acquainted with Hanging Maw, a Cherokee chief who subsequently was with the party who captured her and the Callaway girls.[12]

3

To Kentucky

Lyman Draper: Can you tell me anything about your father's first attempt to settle Kentucky, in 1773?

Nathan Boone: I have some recollections of the Powell Valley defeat, but I don't know how they were formed. The tragedy occurred on the northern bank of Wallen's Creek. My brother, James Boone, was shot through his hips and rendered helpless. The affair was witnessed by a Negro who hid in the driftwood in the creek. He saw Big Jim, a man with very high cheekbones, an unusually broad face, and a peculiar chin, whom he easily recognized. This Indian was well known by the Boone family and spoke broken English. Whether he was a Shawnee or a Cherokee I cannot remember, but father was always inclined to believe that he was a Shawnee.[1] In any event he was frequently seen in the Watauga and Clinch country.

On the night of the murder, Big Jim approached my brother with a tomahawk. James implored him by name to spare him, but Jim paid no regard to these pleas or to the old friendships, for he had been treated kindly by the Boone family.

There were three groups moving to Kentucky, with the leading party being led by my father. Captain [William] Russell's rear party also contained a number of men, but not as many as in the lead party.

Father and Russell must have been previously acquainted, as they had formed this expedition to settle Kentucky. Father had certainly hunted in the area and had been on the Clinch [River] and at Russell's house. Likewise, he was engaged in getting adventurers for this enterprise and had certainly gone to the South Yadkin and engaged some of the Bryans' in-laws to join him.

There was a young fellow whom the others didn't like in the advance party, who finally decided to return. He left the main front camp before daylight and went off unknown to the others. He was the first to come upon the camp of the slain and immediately returned to Father's party with the intelligence. He got there about sunrise. A group was sent back to bury the dead. I cannot say who or how many others were killed. Because of the attack, the main party was in confusion, and a day or two elapsed before they decided to return. I am certain there was no attack by Indians on Father's camp, no repulsing them. And afterwards, they went no farther.[2]

Draper: According to the newspaper accounts of 1773, the cattle were with young James Boone. After the attack, perhaps the men collected the scattered cattle. If there were any cattle with the rear group, they were Russell's. But the fact that Russell's son and two Negroes were with James Boone would indicate that Russell had sent livestock forward under their charge, possibly packhorses with articles as Mrs. Moore says and as Dunmore's speech indicates. But very likely they had cattle also, for Daniel Boone in his narrative said that this misfortune "scattered our cattle." This could only refer to the cattle to the rear, so the defeat probably scattered the stock. The newspaper account says Boone's advance consisted of thirty men, and young Russell's middle detachment had eight, with Captain Russell with the rear. Mrs. Moore and Captain Gass know of only Captains Russell and David Gass in the rear, which would make forty all together.[3] Colonel Daniel Boone in his narrative indicates his own and five other families and forty men.

Olive Boone: James Boone had gone by some mill to get flour or meal and pack it up and overtake the leading party. He was expected the night of October 9.

Nathan Boone: Probably James went both to notify Captain Russell and to get flour. I don't remember anything about his driving any cattle or on which side of Wallen's Creek they were camped.

Olive Boone: I do not remember the name of that creek, but I remember Colonel Daniel and Mrs. Boone said that the young men were camped at the ford and were three miles short of the main camp in front. I also remember the names of the Mendingalls, and I feel pretty certain a young Drake was one of those slain. And that Big Jim was well known to young James Boone and had often visited the Boone family and been kindly entertained and befriended by them. In the attack James Boone was wounded through both hips, which were broken. I think young Russell was wounded in the same manner. When the Indians tortured James Boone, they pulled out his toenails and fingernails. He first begged Big Jim to spare him and finally, when being tortured, to kill him at once and put him out of his misery. Young Russell was tortured in the same way. Finally they were both severely stabbed all to pieces and probably tomahawked, which put them out of their misery.[4]

Nathan Boone: While yet suffering, young Boone said to Russell that he presumed that his mother, brothers, and sisters were all killed by the Indians. This was reported by the Negro who escaped and hid in the driftwood. The young fellow in the front camp had stolen something, so he left just before daybreak and on the way took some deer skins hung up to dry beside the road, which were killed by the front party. They expected James Boone and party would see them and bring them along. He soon came upon the camp of the slain; he left his skins and hastened back, and reached the camp about sunrise. All were alarmed and feared the main camp would be soon be attacked. They set about rudely fortifying themselves, probably using fallen trees. While Squire Boone and several others went back to bury the dead, my mother furnished some sheets for that purpose. James and young Russell were buried in the same grave, wrapped in the same sheet. Michael Stoner was in Father's advance party. As I mentioned, there was no attack on Daniel Boone's camp, no repulse. In fact, there were no Indians seen. The party went no farther, and by general consent all returned.

The next spring, in May, my father went to hunt and to look at the grave. He found the wolves had rolled off the logs from the graves and scratched down into the graves. He decided to dig down with a handspike to investigate and found the bodies. Fresh blood was yet upon their heads. He could easily distinguish them, as his son had fair hair, while young Russell's was black. Both had plaited hair, a frontier custom probably taken from the Indians. While he was still at the grave, having barely refilled the hole and replaced the logs, a sudden storm came up and lasted some time. During this time, the melancholy of his feelings mingled with the howling of the storm and the gloominess of the place made him feel worse than ever in his life. After it became light and cleared off rightly, he went a few hundred yards, hobbled out his horse, made a fire, and lay down, but he could not sleep. He soon heard Indians approaching, who discovered the fire. Unseen, Father stole off, found his horse, and carefully drove him before him, with his bell yet on to deceive the Indians, through some narrows on the creek, and then stopped the bell and made off. He heard no more of the Indians. Father would be noticeably affected when he described this incident. The storm very likely delayed the Indians and thus saved Father's life, presuming they were warlike.

Draper: What can you tell me about the trip to Kentucky with Michael Stoner in 1774?

Nathan Boone: I remember hearing about the time Governor Dunmore of Virginia sent Father and Michael Stoner to Kentucky to recall the surveyors.[5] Stoner was an awkward Dutchman, a low chunky man. He became a good woodsman, as he was truthful and reliable. In later years he hunted in Missouri and stopped at our house; through good circumstances Father was at home. Once an old neighbor of Stoner's from Kentucky came here and said to Stoner, as a ruse to get him to go home, that in Kentucky people thought that he was dead, and his wife was engaged to be married again in the near future. The next morning Michael Stoner packed off for Kentucky.

On the way to Kentucky in 1774, they came upon some small stream at a horseshoe bend. There they found a neck of ground raised to a high narrow ridge or point; on both sides the buffalo had licked until a small hole was worn through the embankments. Seeing this, Stoner went down and discovered a buffalo through the hole on the other side. He said "Stop Captain, and we will have some fun." Stoner slipped forward, and taking his cap off his head, he suddenly thrust the cap through the small hole, which was scarcely larger than the cap itself. The cap was thrust into the buffalo's face while the animal was busily engaged licking the dirt. Instead of scampering back terrified as Stoner had expected, the buffalo angrily forced his head and neck through the clay bank up to his shoulders. Stoner, alarmed for his own safety, wheeled and ran, exclaiming, "Shoot her, Captain! Shoot her, Captain!" My father threw himself upon the ground in a fit of laughter at the ridiculous result of Stoner's exploit, at his expense instead of the buffalo's. After the buffalo caused Stoner's hasty retreat, he seemed content with his success and made no further pursuit.

My father and Stoner continued on their mission and discovered that some of the surveyors had been attacked and dispersed by the Indians. Father also found some of the surveyors and gave them notice of their danger, particularly some at Mann's Lick, a few miles south of the Falls of Ohio.[6] He visited the falls, and in going out on the rocks while the water was low, he found petrified buffalo dung attached to one of the rocks.[7]

Draper: There are some stories that your father visited Harrodsburg while searching for the surveyors, and in Filson's narrative he said he conducted in the surveyors.[8] Did he ever mention going to the mouth of the Kentucky River or to the lick where Boonesboro was built?

Nathan Boone: I cannot say if he actually accompanied any surveyors back to the settlements or not. I have no recollection of my father and Stoner going to the mouth of the Kentucky River or to the Big Lick where Boonesboro was afterwards located or to Harrodstown.

Draper: What have you heard about your father's service during Dunmore's War in 1774?

Nathan Boone: I know very little about my father's military service in 1774, except that he raised a small company and started to march out on the Point Pleasant campaign. They traveled for a day or two, but he was overtaken with orders to return and take command of three forts on the Clinch [River].[9] My father was commissioned captain by Governor Dunmore, as he often said. I have seen and for a time had the commission, but it was sent to Colonel Benton about 1833 or 1834. He wanted to see if any claim could be established in favor of Father for his service within the Virginia line or in Colonel George Rogers Clark's regiment. But he was unable to establish a pension, and the commission never returned.

Olive Boone: I have heard my father and my uncle, Peter and John Van Bibber, say they believed that not more than half the men were actually engaged in the Point Pleasant battle. Many were retained in camp by General Lewis. They said that the Indian line was stretched from the Ohio to the Kanawha.

Nathan Boone: John McKinney, who died in Kentucky about twenty years ago, told me he was at the Point Pleasant battle when only about fifteen years old. The battle began in the morning while it was yet quite foggy, and powder smoke settled and intermingled with the fog, as the sun had not yet dissipated the fog. He was badly wounded in the engagement and rendered helpless; and when several Indians stabbed him, several of the whites rushed up, drove off the Indians, and rescued McKinney. I believe him, as he was trustworthy.[10]

After Dunmore's War, I think Richard Henderson's Transylvania Company got most of their knowledge about the Kentucky country from my father; otherwise they would not have employed him. I heard Father say that he was employed by the company to gather the Indians for the treaty as well as to furnish the meets and bounds of the purchase.[11]

Draper: This is good evidence that Daniel Boone was the principal person whom Henderson consulted for information on Kentucky.

Nathan Boone: My father was to have a certain portion of the new purchase for his services, but the exact amount of land I do not remember. He was also hired to mark the road to Kentucky and to establish a new town for the settlement. All this was duly performed, but his pay fell through with the failure of the Transylvania Company to maintain their claim and purchase. But my father took the loss well and troubled himself no further about it.

I don't remember any of the details about his blazing the Kentucky road except that John Stewart's remains were found and that Thomas Twitty was killed. Of course, there is the story of William Nall's being bitten. He was in camp one night, when a wolf crept up and attempted to bite Nall but was scared or dodged off. The wolf made several repeated attempts, always seeming to aim only at Nall. Finally, the men got Nall to change his position and lie in the center of the group, but even then the wolf jumped in and bit him on the forehead. After that they killed the wolf. Subsequently, during the summer, while fire-hunting on some river with his brother-in-law, Nall was seized with hydrophobia. His brother had to jump out of the canoe. When he recovered, Nall expressed fears that he might bite someone, so he was tied. Later he went into another fit from which he never recovered.

Draper: According to Captain Gass, this seizure occurred on the Clinch River.[12]

Olive Boone: I have no recollection about the wolf incident, but I heard Colonel Daniel Boone say that once alone he saw a wolf coming towards him on a path, and as it did not turn out, he began to suspect it was mad and threw his hat at it, which the wolf seized, and Boone had to shoot the wolf to regain his hat. This happened on a buffalo road between the Blue Licks and the Ohio River while he was exploring the countryside in the summer of 1770. I should mention that I am quite certain that Colonel Boone and his family lived on the Watauga [River] but can recollect nothing to prove it nor the length of time he lived there.

Draper: Did Colonel Boone ever mention hunting at the French Lick on the Cumberland River?[13]

Nathan Boone: Not that I recall. I suppose my father must have moved to the Watauga soon after his return home in 1771, and he remained there until 1772 or possibly 1773. He considered this residence to be on the way to Kentucky. He either sold his farm on the head of the Yadkin [River] before he went to the Watauga, or he went back and sold it in 1773. I suppose it is even possible that he may have moved back to the Yadkin, then sold the farm, and started in September 1773 for Kentucky, but I would think my father tarried a year or so on the Watauga. I have no idea if he owned land, lived as a squatter, or perhaps he leased lands from the Cherokees as mentioned by Haywood.

Draper: What do you know about the first little fort on the Kentucky River, called Fort Boone, and did your sister, Mrs. Susannah Hays, travel to Kentucky in 1775 with the road cutters?[14]

Nathan Boone: I don't remember anything about Fort Boone, nor exactly when Susannah came to Kentucky, but I am inclined to think she did. She was married when Father was living on the Clinch River, and there Hays taught my father to write with an improved hand. He even kept Father's accounts for a while. I always understood that her firstborn, Elizabeth, was the first white child born in Kentucky. Elizabeth married Isaac Van Bibber, whose father, Isaac, was killed at the Point Pleasant battle, and the younger Isaac was a cousin of my wife. Elizabeth was born in 1775 or 1776. One John Anderson, whose parents lived at Boonesboro, was the second [white] child born in Kentucky. My father and mother possibly said they were the first children born at Boonesboro.

Olive Boone: I definitely remember Colonel Daniel Boone and his wife used to speak of them as the first children born on the banks of the Kentucky. Of John Anderson I know nothing more, but Major Van Bibber married Elizabeth Hays in Kentucky and came to Missouri after his wife died, perhaps in the fall of 1830. Her husband died a few years later, about 1845. He lived at Loutre Lick, in Callaway or Montgomery County, where he long kept a public house.

They have two sons and four daughters still living. Isaac Van Bibber is the oldest child, who lives at the old place at Loutre Lick. Ewing Van Bibber went to California. One of the daughters, probably Arretta, married a Burt, and another, Susannah, married a Higgason. They both lived near Loutre Lick. Another daughter, Elgiva, married a Davis, but I do not known where he lives. Matilda married an Estill who went to Carolina and died. She is living as a widow about twelve miles southwest of here.

We used to gather nettles, a sort of hemp, toward spring, and when it became rotted by the wet weather, we would spin them. It was very strong. It grows in rich land about four feet high. Nettles, the warp, and buffalo wool spun the filling—both spun. For socks the buffalo wool alone was used. It was quite soft and wears very well.

We found turkeys were very thin in summer because of ticks and made poor food. In the fall they would fatten rapidly on beech and other small mast. They were good eating in fall, winter, and spring. Buffaloes are best when eaten in the fall, as they feed upon grass, buffalo clover, and pea vine and feed some upon acorns, chestnuts, and beechnuts. The clover is a large white blossom kind and lasts the growing season, but the pea vine does not amount to much until the latter part of summer and early fall. The deer are also fattest in the fall. They live upon the same kind of food as buffalo, and the elk the same. About Christmas they would begin to thin down. They became very poor in the latter part of winter and early spring but in May began to improve. Frontier people probably found no wild bees and honey, as bees do not generally precede white settlements. There were none in the woods of Missouri until after the settlements expanded.

Draper: Did Colonel Boone ever say he met Simon Kenton at the Blue Licks?[15]

Nathan Boone: Not to my knowledge. I always understood from my father that the first time he saw Kenton was when he came to Boonesboro. Simon Kenton lived a year or so at Boonesboro with our family but was then known as Simon Butler. He changed his real name from Kenton in consequence of his supposed killing his companion in a fisticuff fight. Later he learned that his companion did not die, and when Kenton came to make some early land entries, he resumed his given name and made his entries accordingly. My father had great confidence in Kenton as a spy and woodsman. Kenton visited Missouri in the spring or summer of 1805 or 1806 and spent about a week at our house when we lived about twenty-five miles above St. Charles, on the north side of the Femme Osage River and about six miles back from the Missouri. During that visit my father was residing in a small house almost adjoining mine in the same yard. The old pioneers seemed to enjoy themselves finely in recounting their old Kentucky troubles and hardships. Kenton had a son with him, but I don't think they explored the country very much. At that time the area above St. Charles was not much settled.

Draper: Can you tell me about the capture of the girls at Boonesboro in 1776?

Nathan Boone: The girls went pleasuring in a canoe on Sunday. One of the Callaway girls wanted to go to a certain point to get some young cane, and my sister, Jemima Boone, was steering the canoe.[16] As the canoe touched shore, Indians leaped out and seized the girls, and the Callaway girls fought with their paddles. Jemima used to say she then had a sore foot, from a cane stab, and had got the other girls to go to the river with her that she might hold her foot in the water to quiet the pain.

After capture, the Indians hurried the girls away. A few miles off,

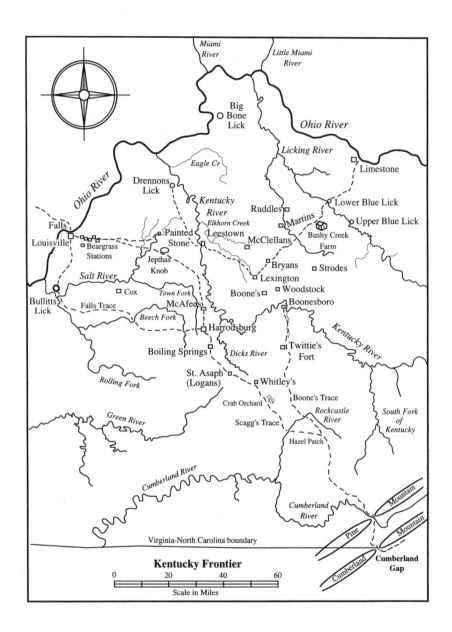

Kentucky Frontier

Scale in Miles

0   20   40   60

the Indians had left an old white horse. While the Indians hurried the girls, they delayed as much as possible. The Indians then cut off the girls' dresses and petticoats to the knees to speed their progress and gave them moccasins and leggings. Hanging Maw, a Cherokee, was of the group. Jemima Boone knew him, probably having met him when living on the Watauga. He asked if all were daughters of Daniel Boone. She said yes, feeling they would be treated more kindly. Hanging Maw then said laughingly, "We have done pretty well for old Boone this time."

When they reached the horse, they put Jemima on it first because of her sore foot and occasionally put all three girls on together. The horse was cross and would bite. The girls did everything they could to make a trail by dropping bits of cloth, etc., until the Indians put a stop to it.

When first captured, their screams were heard. Father was lying down on the bed at his house, and jumped up and seized his gun and started off without his moccasins.

Olive Boone: Colonel Daniel Boone always said he got no moccasins till the Indians were defeated, when some were found in their packs.

Nathan Boone: The only person I definitely recall being in the pursuing party was Flanders Callaway. Colonel Richard Callaway started with the pursuers, and they soon found the Indian trail. Callaway was for following directly on the trail, but Father objected; I suppose Colonel Callaway then returned to Boonesboro. The reason my father objected to following the trail was if the Indians had a back watch, the pursuers would be discovered. This would give the Indians time enough to tomahawk the girls. He reasoned that a better way would be to fall in ahead and strike and watch their warpaths.

The first night someone had to return for supplies. I think there were two or three; and very likely Colonel Callaway had returned as soon as the Indian trail was discovered and their direction determined. Father's advice was followed. The party bore off to one side of their route, and on the day the girls were retaken, they again found the Indian trail. This they followed a short distance, where they found a dead buffalo. The Indians had killed and skinned a part of the hump, cut out a piece, and pushed on.

They only took part, as the whole hump would often weigh two hundred pounds. It was in a set of strong bones from one to two feet high, which shoot up from the back or shoulder bones, and on each side of this row of bones, there is a hundredweight of meat, and sometimes more, that can be a cut of delicious meat. Then the range of hump bones cut out and roasted as a spare rib is very delicious.

When father saw that the buffalo had just been killed and the blood was yet trickling down, he was certain the Indians would stop to cook when they reached the first water. Later they found a small snake the Indians had killed, which was still writhing in death. Then they discovered the Indian party had separated. The white men also split into two groups to search for the Indians both up and down the stream. Father, with the right-hand party, had gone about two or three hundred yards, and when descending a hill into a glen, they saw the Indians camped at a small branch. Immediately my father and some others shot at them and then rushed the camp.

The girls were sitting in the grass on the ground in a small open glade and a few steps from the fire and were apparently guarded by one of the Indians in a reclining posture. The fire was kindled, and three other Indians were gathering wood and preparing for cooking, while another Indian was posted some distance in the rear. This fellow, seeing from the smoke that the fire was kindled, left his gun standing and ran down to light his pipe, and had reached the fire when Boone and party fired; or so my sister always said. At the crack of the guns, the girls jumped up, Jemima shouted, "That's Daddy," and started towards their rescuers. Father yelled to them to throw themselves flat upon the ground in case the Indians might shoot back or [in case they might] accidentally get harmed by the shots of the whites. The girls obeyed. The men did not know how many Indians there were, or if more than they saw might not be nearby. One of the Indians at the fire was shot and fell into the fire. He must have risen and run off mortally wounded, as nothing particularly was said about it. This Indian who was shot at the fire was probably the one shot by John Floyd. Father then pointed out the bush where the Indian stood that he shot, and there found the Indian's rifle.

The girls had been expecting to be rescued until that day but had finally given up hope and were very downhearted. The Indians gave them jerked meat, but Jemima said she never felt like eating a morsel. But her foot mended during the captivity travel. When attacked, the Indians made no attempt to injure the girls. I think that Flanders Callaway was with the party to the left, and he was a little later than Boone's party in discovering the Indians' camp. One of this group fired a long shot.[17] Jemima Boone was born October 4, 1762 and was in her thirteenth year when captured. It was not long after that she married young, to Flanders Callaway.

Draper: What have you heard about the attack at Boonesboro on April 24, 1777?

Nathan Boone: Two men went out to hunt or drive up horses or something and were fired on at the head of the lane. They were about four hundred yards from the fort, and Daniel Goodman was killed, but the other escaped.[18] Before he got in the fort, Father with a party rushed out the gate, and before they reached the dead man, they were fired on from the fence corners of the fields on either side of the lane. Afterward there was some skirmishing as they returned to the fort. During the retreat my father and two or three others were wounded. My father was shot through the left ankle, which broke the bone. The ball was mashed as thin as a knife blade when it was drawn out from the opposite side from where it entered. His daughter Jemima, seeing him coming back wounded, ran out and met him several rods from the fort and assisted him in, he leaning upon her.[19] Thereafter, when fatigued, he would feel pain from this wound.

The Indians stayed around the fort for two days, skirmishing. Father had a painful time with his broken ankle. He had his leg placed in a swing as he lay in bed during his recovery. Mother used to speak of this as the first attack on Boonesboro and as lasting two days. She said the second attack, on May 23 until the morning of May 25, lasted three days, and the third and last attack in September 1778 lasted nine days. She always thus designated them and made no allusion to any of the lesser affairs that occurred at Boonesboro.[20]

· 4 ·

CAPTURED BY INDIANS

Lyman Draper: Tell us about Colonel Boone being made a captive at the Blue Licks in February 1778. I believe in his narrative it says he was taken February 7 and surrendered the men the next day.

Nathan Boone: I think it was Saturday when my father was taken and Sunday when he surrendered up the others.[1] He said he went out on horseback to kill meat for the company. The buffalo seldom visited the licks in the winter; they then would keep near the cane as the best winter's range and lived in summer mainly on grass. I remember that region. I went from Kanawha to attend school near Lexington for about eighteen months during 1793 and 1794. At that time the nearest cane of consequence to the Lower Blue Licks was about five or six miles off, in the rich cane lands towards Mays Lick.[2] But I actually don't know if Father was hunting in that direction or the exact distance he was from the Blue Licks. But in any event he had killed a buffalo and loaded his horse with meat. It had started snowing quite hard before he killed the buffalo, so he started for the licks, which he had left that morning. He had proceeded some distance when he discovered a small party of Indians on his trail. The snow was now something like an inch or so deep, and he could easily be followed. Father at once attempted to untie and throw off the load of meat, but failed because the fresh buffalo strings were frozen. These strings had been cut from the buffalo that made up his heavy load, perhaps three hundred or four hundred pounds, and lashed around the horse's belly by the tugs.

Then he attempted to draw his knife from the scabbard to cut the tugs, but he found his knife, which had been thrust into the sheath when all bloody, had frozen. Father's greasy hands and greasy knife handle prevented him from getting the knife out.

By this time the Indians were very close, and he could not get his horse unloaded on which to escape. Thus his only chance was to dart off on foot. After running about half a mile or thereabouts, the Indians approached close and commenced firing at him. Father believed they did not intend to kill him, as several balls struck on either side of him close by, knocking up the snow. They then came within eight or ten paces and fired another volley. One ball cut the strap of his powder horn loose. He believed that if they had wished, they might easily have killed him.

Eventually he was too tired to run farther, and as the Indians were gaining on him, he decided that it would be impossible to escape. He then dodged behind a tree and placed his gun by the side of the tree, leaning against it in plain view, as a token of surrender. The Indians came up whooping and laughing, in view of their success, and took his gun, knife, and ammunition. I do not know of any conversation occurring here. The Indians then changed their course and in almost three miles came to a large body of Indians and several Frenchmen. Two of the latter were officers; the only names of the party I remember are Black Fish, Captain Will, the Negro interpreter Pompey, Laramie, and Baubee. Pompey spoke good Indian as well as English. I don't know how or when he joined the Indians.

My father, Colonel Daniel Boone, used to say that in his early Indian troubles and difficulties in Kentucky, if he dreamed of his father and he was angry, it would forebode evil; but if he appeared pleasant, he had nothing to fear. Each time when captured, robbed or defeated, he thus dreamed unfavorably about his father.[3]

On arriving at their camp he was taken to Black Fish, the principal chief, where several other Indians soon gathered. My father recognized his old captor of 1769, so he went up and shook hands with him. Father greeted him with "How d'do, Captain Will?" The Indian asked where he had known him; Father asked him if he did not remember taking two men prisoner eight years ago on the Kentucky River. Captain Will then recognized him and renewed the shaking of hands with great cordiality, and several others now came up as familiarly as though they had also previously known him. A most ludicrous scene of handshaking and mock friendship ensued, with all apparent sincerity and gravity on the part of these forest warriors. Father took it all with grace and politeness, of which he was master.

Using Pompey as an interpreter, Black Fish asked my father about his men who were at Pe-Me-Mo Lick. This was the general name in Shawnee for salt springs, referring to the Lower Blue Licks. Father asked how they knew his men were there, and they said their spies had seen them. Father then admitted those men were his, and Black Fish informed him they were going there to kill them. My father then proposed, if they would not mistreat them nor make them run the gauntlet, he would surrender them up as prisoners of war.

This the Indians agreed to. I think my father's reason for surrendering his men was knowing that with several inches of snow upon the ground, if attacked none would be able to escape, [as the Indians could follow their trails in the snow]. The enemy had four times as many men as the salt boilers, and the latter, ignorant of their presence, would find it impossible to escape. He also knew the next day was Sunday, so when the Indians arrived, his men would be loitering about and off their guard. Moreover, it being midwinter, they would not be dreaming of an Indian in the country.

Draper: Do you think his surrender was to divert the Indians from going against Boonesboro?

Nathan Boone: I don't know. My father used to say he knew they were going against Boonesboro, but I think he only judged it from circumstances. About noon on the next day, the Indians arrived near the Blue Licks, and Father was escorted by a number of Indians to the hill on the south side of Licking River, directly opposite the salt spring.[4]

Draper: Which of the springs?

Nathan Boone: I suppose it was the one on the north side of the river. The salt makers were lying about on their blankets apparently sunning themselves with the snow then half a leg deep. My father called out to the men that they were surrounded by a large body of Indians. He explained that he had stipulated for their surrender and had secured the promise of good treatment for them. He said that it was impossible for them to get away and begged them not to attempt to defend themselves, as they would all be massacred. They at once yielded to his advice; and as my father and the Indians with him began to descend the hill, the others began to come in from every direction.

I don't think the Indians camped at the licks that night. I believe that they went on towards the Ohio a few miles before they camped. What was done with the salt they had made I do not recall. Three men had already left with some salt, and twenty-seven surrendered. I think Flanders Callaway was one who had gone back. I have no knowledge of any council held at the Blue Licks, as Joe Jackson says, or none anywhere of such a nature as Jackson represents.[5] I know the Indians took some of the kettles and the axes.

That night when camped, the Indians began to clear snow and make a road about a hundred yards long. Pompey told my father it was for running the gauntlet. My father reminded Black Fish of his promise not to make the prisoners run the gauntlet. Black Fish told him it was not for his men, who had capitulated, but for himself, who had been captured and had made no such stipulation.

Black Fish said he could run the gauntlet there immediately or wait till he reached the Indian towns. Father chose to run the gauntlet immediately. The line was formed. Some of the Indians had clubs or sticks, and some had tomahawks. And Father ran. The Indians made great motions as if they would split his brains out but seemed to favor him; he only received a few slight strokes from switches.

The same evening a dispute arose as to whether to trim the ears of the prisoners, that is, to split the rim of the ear fully two inches in length in which, when healed, to hang bobs and things as was the Indian custom. The two French officers argued this point, one for and one against. They became so heated that they drew swords against each other. The Indians prevented bloodshed.

At the time my father asked Pompey what this was about, and Pompey told him. This proposal of trimming the prisoners' ears must have been the thing that Joe Jackson was talking about when he said a council was held to determine the fate of the prisoners. But possibly there may have been a council held, and my father may have spoken in it in behalf of the prisoners and demanded the fulfillment of the stipulations and that Jackson misunderstood the point discussed.

I think the return march of the Indians to the Shawnee towns was one of severity and want, and I heard that some of the Indians had their ears frozen. I have heard my father speak of the want of food and of eating slippery elm bark (rather loosening) and then oak bark ooze by chewing to counteract any bad effects. The Indians have what they call black drink made into a soup with weeds (what it is made of I do not know), which they take when they have overloaded their stomachs at a dog feast when they have tried to see who could eat the most and wish to vomit. But I cannot say either occurred on this march. I cannot say what route they used or the place where they crossed the Ohio, but I know some were made to carry the heavy salt kettles.

Eventually Black Fish and others took my father to Detroit. Governor [Henry] Hamilton offered to ransom him, but Black Fish refused.[6] He probably wanted to make use of him for the peaceable surrender of Boonesboro. At the first arrival of Black Fish, Hamilton discovered that my father was the principal prisoner and sent for him. He wished to keep and entertain him that night, and return him next morning. The governor wanted to gain intelligence; he had my father in his room and inquired if he had heard anything of Burgoyne's army. Father replied, "Yes, it is well known in Kentucky as a fact before I was taken that Burgoyne and his whole army have surrendered to General Gates." Governor Hamilton then called to his private secretary, John Hay, in an adjoining room, and said, "Hay, the report of Burgoyne's disaster, I fear, is too true; Captain Boone says it was well known in Kentucky before he was taken." Feeling convinced of it, Hamilton requested my father not to mention it to the Indians, as it would do no good. My father replied, "You are too late, Governor. I have already told them of it."

The governor then desired that my father speak slightingly of the affair, as if it were merely a vague report and was unworthy of belief— that he had jokingly spoken of it. I do not remember hearing of any other conversation.

When the governor found that the Indians would not give up my father, he gave orders to the king's commissary to furnish him with a horse, saddle, bridle, and blanket and also with a quantity of Indian silver trinkets to use among the Indians as currency. The horse furnished was a pony. I think it very likely that my father used some policy with Hamilton, but I do not know if he exhibited his Dunmore commission.

Returning from Detroit, Black Fish went down the lake and up

Huron River to visit the Mingoes and other Indian towns, then came upon the heads of Scioto and down it, visiting other Indian towns.[7] He gave them all notice to assemble for the giant expedition against Kentucky.

The first salt boiler to escape and reach the settlements was Andrew Johnson. He had convinced the Indians he was a fool, afraid of guns, afraid to leave camp by himself, etc. The Indians made sport of him and, as he was small, named him Pe-Cu-La, meaning "the little duck." Actually, he was an admirable woodsman, and on an early occasion he ran off.[8]

Johnson soon reached Boonesboro and piloted a small party to the Indian country near Chillicothe. He attacked several sugar camps which adjoined each other and defeated the Indians at the camps, perhaps killing one or more; then he returned safely back to Boonesboro. I have no idea what subsequently became of Johnson.

Black Fish asked my father who he thought could have done this bold act. He answered, more to annoy the Indians than really believing it, that it was Pe-Cu-La. Black Fish said it could not have been because Pe-Cu-la was a fool and could never have reached Kentucky. My father said he was no fool and was a fine woodsman. "Then why did you not tell me so before," inquired Black Fish. "Because you never asked me," Father answered. Upon his return to Boonesboro he learned that it really had been Johnson who incited and piloted the expedition against the sugar camps.

This raid gave the Indians much concern, as unimportant as it was, it being the very first enterprise of the Kentuckians against their towns, and was the first proof to them that the captivity of the large party of salt boilers was in a fair way to result as disastrously to the Indians as advantageously to the whites.

Samuel Brooks and James Callaway attempted to run off from the Detroit region in a canoe.[9] They started down the Detroit River in a fog, but as it cleared off, they found themselves in the very midst of an Indian town on the bank of the stream and were retaken. They were made to run the gauntlet and run past squaws and children and youngsters, who are always more unmerciful to one running the gauntlet than men are. Both passed through a severe ordeal, particularly Brooks, who when struck would stop and strike the Indians in return and during the race got his arm broken. They were put in confinement and were overheard planning another attempt to escape. Brooks had to talk loud as Callaway was hard of hearing. Thus their design was thwarted. Brooks died in captivity, and my father used to say that probably Brooks would have survived and returned but for his irascible conduct and getting himself constantly embroiled in difficulties.

I do not recall how James Callaway got away. He settled in Missouri, in Howard County, and probably has children living. One, named Stephen, was in Platte or Buchanan County. James Callaway has been dead fifteen or twenty years. He came to Missouri several years after the Boone family. He was the brother of Flanders and Micajah Callaway.[10]

Jess Cofer, another of the captives, subsequently returned to Boonesboro. He married a daughter of Samuel Boone, the brother of my father, Daniel Boone, and settled and died in Kentucky, probably in Clark County.[11]

Another was Nathaniel Bullock, not Nathan Bullit, as Kenton has it. That was the name, as I have often heard it. I don't know what became of him.[12]

There is a story of Black Fish having my father fell a tree and cut notches in it to hold about a quart for salting the horses. In doing this job he blistered his hands, then showed them to Black Fish, into whose family he had been adopted. Father told him he was being treated like a slave instead of a son; he said he had servants to do such work in Kentucky. Black Fish then excused him from further labor.

Both Black Fish and his squaw treated Father very kindly, and he seemed to think much of them. They had two daughters, both small, named Pom-Me-Pe-Sy and Pim-Me-Pe-Sy. The former was four or five years old, ill-tempered and hateful; the youngest was a mere child, perhaps a year old, with a kind temper, and Boone used to nurse it frequently. He used the silver trinkets as currency and would buy maple sugar and give it to the children, who would smilingly call it "molas."

An example of Black Fish's kindness and an Indian's idea of taste was that Black Fish would suck a lump of sugar a while in his mouth, take it out, and give it to Boone, whom he always addressed as "my son." Black Fish at that time was perhaps fifty years old but perhaps not quite that old. Black Fish gave my father the name Shel-Tow-Y, which meant "the Big Turtle."

Once my father asked Black Fish for permission to hobble his pony and turn it out to pasture when the spring grass came up. Black Fish made him wait a while, then gave permission. In the meantime he had armed men hide flat in the grass to see if he would try to get away. My father pretended not to see them and gave no cause for suspicion. This happened two or three times, but finally he was allowed the liberty. He could have escaped much sooner than he did but wanted to learn more definitely about the expedition against Boonesboro.

Once my father's pony was missing, and Black Fish would do nothing about it. Father knew the Indians had a habit of "borrowing" from each other without asking permission and would not give each other away if the owner complained. He only feared the pony would not be returned in time for his escape effort.

Finally the pony was returned but had been badly used; its back was very sore. Care and attention soon restored it. My father would occasionally help his Indian mother hoe corn. Black Fish would tell him he need not work, that his mother could easily raise enough for all of them. Black Fish would also smooth out dirt and mark out the geography of the country, apparently to amuse my father. In shooting at a mark Father would suffer the Indians to beat him that they might not be jealous. Soon he was permitted to hunt alone.

William Hancock, who was a very poor woodsman and discontented with his captivity and moody, didn't see how my father could be whistling and contented among the dirty Indians when he was so melancholy.[13] The worst act the Indians ever did, Father used to say, was taking their salt kettles or showing them the way to their towns and the geography of the Indian country. That resulted in a later attack by the Kentuckians, though at first they deemed their capture so great a disaster.

Black Fish and his wife and a party went to the Scioto Licks and saltworks to make salt and took my father with them. It was probably at the Paint Creek town where Jimmy Rogers lived. He was a white man prisoner who never abandoned the Shawnees and finally moved with those that went to Missouri. He first lived at Owen's Station, twelve miles nearly west of St. Louis, and afterwards moved onto the creek called the Burbees, which runs into the Merimack River and within three miles of where a village of Xenia now is. He raised an Indian family, and some of his children were educated. He got Father to exercise his skill in gun making to stock a gun for him, which he did. An Indian also got him to stock a rifle barrel. My father took it with him and did it in a rough substantial manner while at the salt licks. When Father escaped he was at first greatly afraid he had carried the gun he had stocked for him but later found it.

My father, Daniel Boone, had previously concealed some powder and ball from the supply given him for hunting. It was the second day on the way to Chillicothe from the salt licks, near night, and the Indians scared up a flock of turkeys. They chased them some distance before they lighted in trees. While the Indians were busily engaged in shooting them, all the Indians had left, and father was alone with the horses, squaws, and children. It was at that time he decided he would start for Kentucky. By then the Indian army had begun to assemble. He cut the ropes and threw off the load of brass kettles. His Indian mother saw this and asked what he was going to do. He said he was going to see his wife. She said he must not do so for Black Fish would be angry. He mounted his pony and laid on the whip as the squaws raised a loud holloo to give the alarm. But he was soon beyond hearing. Jimmy Rogers said that the Indians followed his trail some distance and returned, saying he would get lost. But Rogers said he knew better—that he was sure my father would go straight as a leather string home.

My father rode hard that evening and all night until about ten o'clock next morning, when the pony gave out. He had stopped for a few minutes and found the creature's legs became so stiff he could scarcely move them. He then took off the saddle, bridle, and saddle blanket and hung them up in a tree and went on foot as rapidly as he could. The same day he crossed the Ohio. I think my father struck the Ohio a little above Maysville. He found a couple of dry logs, very likely a standing dry sapling, nearly rotted at the roots, and tied them together with a grapevine. He then placed his gun and clothes upon it and swam over, pushing his raft before him. The first night after crossing the Ohio, he was weary and ventured to sleep. He took off his moccasins as usual, wrapped himself in a blanket, and went to sleep. Later he was awakened by something seizing one of his toes and thought the Indians had him again. He jumped up and judged it was a wolf or fox by the noise it made in scampering off. Soon his feet became scalded by heat while walking, so he peeled some oak bark, ground it up, and made some ooze, which he used to wash his feet, then proceeded. The last day after passing the Blue Licks, he killed a buffalo, then cooked and ate a delicious meal. He cut out the tongue, which he carried along to present to his son Daniel, whom he expected to find at Boonesboro.

Olive Boone: I remember what Colonel Boone, then a captain, told me about his capture. It was Saturday when Boone went out to hunt, a cloudy day looking like snow. He killed his meat and loaded his horse, and in going through some narrows beside a stream, then snowing very hard, he passed between a large tree and an upturned root, and the Indians seized and took him. The Indian camp was not far off, where they had a long fire. Captain Boone then went up and shook hands with all of them. Captain Will was near the last when Boone accosted him by name. They all looked surprised at this. Captain Will asked him where he had known him. He answered "Don't you recollect taking two prisoners eight years ago on the Kentucky River? I am one of them, the Big Turtle." He then recognized Captain Boone, and Captain Will setting the example, they all shook hands over again.

I don't remember that anything was said about Indians going against Boonesboro nor of spies reporting discovering the salt boilers. Those men who were captured later were to be well treated and not to run the gauntlet. I have no memory of the council mentioned by Joe Jackson, but I did hear about the proposed ear trimming. Captain Boone did not run the gauntlet at Blue Licks but somewhere on the way to the Indian town. When Captain Boone learned of it, he asked Black Fish, who said Boone had capitulated for the exemption of his men—not for himself. Boone was not hurt. I don't remember particularly anything farther.

Nathan Boone: I remember an event that created a laugh among the Indians. It was the zigzag way my father ran the gauntlet so they could not hit him, but he ran over and knocked down one Indian.

As Father often said, at the Indian town he had promised to surrender Boonesboro and move the people north to the British and Indian country; and while hoeing corn with his Indian mother, Black Fish said, "You need not hoe corn—your mother easily can make enough both for my family and yours also when you bring them out."

Filson quotes my father, Daniel Boone, as saying, "he left the Indians before sunrise, in a secret manner and had witnessed the Indian army assembled at Chillicothe."[14] I am positive that it is a mistake. I feel confident Filson has taken many liberties and made not a few misrepresentations in the narrative, either purposely or unintentionally; and I think their frequency can only be explained by supposing that my father narrated his Kentucky adventures to Filson, who wrote them down from memory at some subsequent period. Much of the language is not my father's.[15]

5

SIEGE OF BOONESBORO

Nathan Boone: Getting back to my story. After his return to Boonesboro, my father, Daniel Boone, went to repairing the fort. The men enlarged it, as the palisades were entirely down on one side. The roofs of the houses were in shed style, all in the same direction, slanting into the fort.[1]

Another escaped prisoner soon came in, reporting that the Indians were delaying their attack two weeks because of my father's escape and had sent an express to Governor Hamilton. When the settlers heard of this postponement, they delayed repairing the fort. It was then that my father carried on the Paint Creek expedition. Upon their return they passed the Indian army at the Lower Blue Licks and hastened on to Boonesboro. After they returned they hastened to complete the repairs, and it was perhaps two or three days before the Indians appeared. In a general way, they never travel far in a day, their armies usually being late in getting breakfast and getting started.

The Indian army arrived, consisting of four hundred Indians and about forty Frenchmen.[2] Pompey came forward and asked for my father. He said Black Fish wished to see him and had letters from Governor Hamilton. So my father and one or two others went out to meet with Black Fish at a stump about sixty yards away.

My father read the letters, which advised him to surrender the fort, as it was impossible to defend themselves against such a force as was going against them. If they attempted to defend the fort, the men, women, and children would probably all be massacred, but if they surrendered the fort, none should be hurt. They would be safely conveyed to Detroit; if any of their property was lost because of the surrender, it should be made good to them. Those who held office should have the same rank under the British government.

Lyman Draper: Did Colonel Boone ever mention the Indians holding up bushes to shade them from the sun during this conference?

Nathan Boone: Not to me. But he told Black Fish he couldn't give him an answer at that time, as many others had come to Boonesboro since he left and there were a number of officers to consult, that he would meet with Black Fish again next morning. Black Fish told my father that his people were hungry and had nothing to eat. My father knew the Indians would most likely kill all the cattle they wished and, preferring to make a show of generosity, said, "There you see a plenty of cattle. Kill what you need and take what corn you want, but don't let any be wasted." The Indians commenced immediately whooping and yelling about, with some shooting down beeves and others cutting down corn.

That night as the cattle came up around the fort, the settlers began getting them inside the walls. Everyone in the fort was decidedly in favor of resistance. But to gain time, it was resolved to ask further time for consideration. My father went out and asked the Indians for another day to reach a decision. The Indians agreed. The following morning Black Fish and my father met again, and Boone told him that the people had decided not to surrender while there was a man living. Black Fish seemed surprised and said Governor Hamilton would be very disappointed, as he had expected the surrender but had ordered the Indians, in case they would not surrender, not to massacre them. He then proposed to hold a friendly treaty and march home. I think the following day was the one appointed for the treaty. Black Fish said he had many chiefs from many different towns with him and that all would have to participate in the treaty. My father said there were so many officers in the fort, more than there actually were, and they all would have to participate.

The number of whites was still less than the number of Indians. The flat, green field in front of the fort was designated for the treaty ground. The only names of whites at the treaty that I remember were Father and Uncle Squire. The articles were proposed and agreed to. The Indians were to return home and the Ohio was to be the boundary, which was not to be passed by either party in a hostile manner.

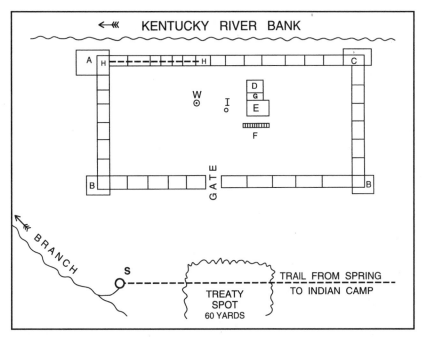

Copy of Moses Boone's sketch of Fort Boonesborough. A–Henderson's kitchen; B–Two-story bastion; C–Phelp's house; D–Squire Boone's house; E–Col. Callaway's house; F–Ball battery; G–Boone's gun shop; H–Ditch or countermine; I–Flagstaff; W–Well; S–Sulphur spring and freshwater spring near together.

This council was to be closed by handshaking, with two Indians to each white man. Then one Indian locked his right arm with a white man's left and with his left hand shook the white man's left; and the other Indian in the same manner on the white man's right. Black Fish was one of those who shook hands with my father. But treachery took place, and a scuffle ensued. Father threw Black Fish flat on the ground, and the other Indian let go his hold. At this instant the other Indian who seems to have carried the pipe tomahawk around for smoking in the council now aimed a blow at Father. He partly dodged the blow, but the handle struck over the back of his head, cutting through the skin. The wound was over two inches long and left a scar over which hair didn't grow. It appeared from the scar that he was leaning in a bending posture in front, as the blade cut a lesser wound between his shoulders, but he then escaped.

Meanwhile, those on guard in the fort began to fire as Indians attempted to drag off the white treaty makers. This seemed to confuse and alarm the Indians, and all the whites escaped. Uncle Squire Boone was wounded in the retreat. Uncle Squire was nine times wounded during the Indian wars. As Father used to say, it was this timely volley from the fort that saved the whites in council; and it was his opinion that when he threw Black Fish down, the other Indians thought he had fallen from a shot from the fort, and this, Father thought, probably added to their dismay and confusion.

Once inside the fort, Father had his wound dressed and went to giving orders. When the firing began there was a Dutchman hiding under Mrs. Stephen Hancock's bed. She reported this to Father, who drove him out of the cabin, and he then jumped into the new well, which had only been dug down a few feet. Father ordered him to go aid in the defense of the fort, but he pleaded he was a potter, not a fighter. Father then ordered him to go to work in the well with a spade and pick. This was at the commencement of the attack. This was the way my father used to relate the incident.

The first day Indians rushed the fort and attempted to scale the walls but were beaten back. They made frequent attempts to set fire to the fort at night by carrying the fire under a blanket, and several got killed in this way. They also tried to fire the fort by shooting torches on their arrows, but the roofs of nearly all the houses along the wall of the fort being sloped inward, the torches could easily be removed by sweeping them off with poles. A second attempt was made to storm the fort but was repulsed. Squire Boone made a wooden cannon, which he fired.[3]

I should mention that the Indians attempted to dig a tunnel into the fort, and the defenders had a countertunnel.[4] My sister Jemima Boone was struck by a spent ball, which was removed without difficulty. I do not recall any particulars of Pompey's being killed, but an Indian peering his head in the fork of a stump was shot from the fort, but I don't know how or by whom. A white man and a Negro were killed in the fort during the siege. David Bundrin was shot in the forehead and died the third day when apparently all his brain ran out of the wound. He rocked his body all the while with his elbow on his knees in a sitting posture but never spoke a word. He sometimes wiped away the oozing-out brains with his hand.

The Negro had dug a hole under the sill of his house and was crawling partially out to get good shots at the Indians during the night. But they located him by flashes of his gun and crept up and tomahawked him. I think they carried off his head as a trophy.[5]

William Hays, my sister's husband, had accompanied my mother and children and his wife to North Carolina and returned immediately and took part in the siege. He saw an Indian at some distance securely posted behind a stump, sitting upon the ground, and shooting frequently with one of his knees exposed to view. Hays said he would try to hit that fellow's knee and shot and wounded the Indian. He broke the knee and splintered up one of the thigh bones, as was afterward learned, and that this was Black Fish.[6] The Indian lived some time, perhaps weeks, and finally died of the wounds.

The Indians retired gradually as though they did not wish to go all at once. After the siege a few dead bodies of the enemy were found around the fort. Some were deposited in rocks and crevices some little distance off and yet others at a greater distance.

My father, Daniel Boone, was considered by the Indians and British as the leading character in the Kentucky country, which was why they conducted their dealings with him.

Olive Boone: I don't recall whether or not it was night when Boone reached Boonesboro after captivity, but he was much disappointed to find his family had gone back to North Carolina. The family cat, which had deserted the house when Mrs. Boone left, returned there half an hour after Daniel Boone's return. Otherwise, the information already given by Nathan is the same as I always heard.

When Jemima received the spent ball in her back, she was dressed only in her underclothes and petticoat. The ball drove the cloth into the fleshy part of the back, but the cloth was not broken, so the ball was easily pulled out by pulling the cloth out. Bundrin, the man who was killed, was a Dutchman. His wife did not realize how badly he was injured and kept saying it was a God's blessing he hadn't been hit in the eye.

I don't recall any details of Pompey's death either, but neither Nathan nor I ever believed Peck's story that Daniel Boone killed him.[7] After the siege it was discovered by watching the buzzards that quite a number of the enemy's dead were thrown into a sort of cave over the Kentucky River. I don't remember the particulars of the death of the Negro, whose name was London. Of the court of inquiry, we know nothing.[8]

Mrs. Boone and family, except Jemima, who was married, and William Hays and his wife, went to North Carolina during Captain Boone's captivity. Evidently he went for his family after the siege.

Nathan Boone: I think he got there in the fall; he would not come out that fall, as it would be too late. The early part of the next season, the Bryans, some of whom were Tories, might have used their influence to prevail upon my mother not to return to the dangers and exposures of Kentucky. She may have well opposed it herself aside from any such influences and so did not move back very soon. Exactly when they returned I do not know.[9]

Draper: Your family moved back to Kentucky in the fall of 1779.

Nathan Boone: I remember that Father had a swivel given him, but I do not know much about it.[10] I can't tell you the particulars of the time and events of his settling Boone's Station, but its locality was on the northeast side of a small stream, a fork of Boone Creek, about half a mile east or northeast of Athens, then called the Cross Plains. There was a large stone mansion on the locality previous to 1799. I know nothing of the size of the fort nor the names of the occupants. Father said that they would see buffalo on the opposite side of the little stream from the fort.

Draper: Did your father ever mention the time he was robbed?

Olive Boone: Oh yes.

Nathan Boone: Father had some friends in his company. They stopped at a tavern to spend the night in some small village in Virginia. They were placed in the chamber, with all to sleep in the same room. They took up their saddlebags with them, and in the morning the saddlebags were found at the foot of the stairs. My father was robbed of the money with which he was going to enter land warrants for himself and others. His other valuables were also gone. No clue could then be found, but a small amount of the money was afterwards discovered in some bottles in the cellar of the house where the robbery occurred. It was my father's opinion that the landlord was the chief plotter of the scheme, and that an old white woman was the instrument, and that she must have hidden in the room, either under the bed or elsewhere, as the door was fastened when Father and his companion retired to rest. The door was found open the next morning. Afterward my father returned to Kentucky. Some who had given money to him with which to purchase warrants forgave him the debt, if debt it could be called. They considered it as an accident that happened to their agent, for which he was not morally responsible. But others demanded repayment of the money. It was a heavy loss to him.[11]

Draper: Did your father tell you about his experiences on Clark's campaign in 1780?

Nathan Boone: No, I know nothing of his being on it. But I was told that Jack Dunn, one of the salt boiler prisoners, deserted from the whites on some campaign and gave the Indians notice.[12]

Also Martin Wetzel escaped from the Indians and reached some station in Kentucky, where he was suspected of being a spy and became quite alarmed. A council was called and my father served on it.

Draper: Did he speak about the death of his brother Edward?

Nathan Boone: I am quite certain my father and his brother went to hunt buffalo meat. I think from the locality it was most likely the Upper Blue Licks where they had been. They had their horses loaded with buffalo meat and stopped at the lick, probably for a rest. They were probably leading their horse or horses and had been just stopped a very few minutes, with the lick close at hand. While Father was cracking some black walnuts, Edward saw a deer enter the lick, and stole up and shot the deer and dragged the carcass into the shade nearby. Some Indians who had probably been watching the lick from a canebrake then shot Edward dead.

My father then jumped on a horse and attempted to throw off the load of meat, but the Indians rushed him, so that he had to abandon the horse and dash off into the canebrake. In the bustle he lost his large, cheap, one-bladed pocketknife, which he had in his hand picking out walnut meats, which probably fell into the creek. The Indians chased him into the cane. The Indians had a dog, and Father shot twice at him. Once or twice the dog ran back, and the Indians would sic him on Father again. Finally he shot the dog, and he was confident the Indians never followed him any farther. I think it was two or three miles that the Indians and their dog chased him, and that the entire distance was a canebrake.

In 1822 some people found this knife with "D. Boone" and the year it was purchased engraved on the handle. It was sent to me, and in 1842 I gave it to Dr. Edward Macomb of the U.S. Army, who wished to deposit it in some eastern museum. The doctor was raised in New York City and was probably a brother of General Macomb. He settled there to practice and since died. Judge Roberts in Kentucky says the knife is in the historic cabinet at Washington.

In consequence of Edward Boone's being killed, there is how Boone Creek and Boone's Lick received their names.[13]

Olive Boone: They did stop just above the lick, but it was Edward who was cracking nuts and Daniel went to the lick. He shot a deer or a buffalo and was butchering it when the Indians fired and killed Edward. I don't remember hearing about the horse. Colonel Boone fled on foot through the cane all the way, and there was only one dog. I have heard Colonel Boone speak of the incident several times.

Draper: Tell me about your father being captured by Colonel Tarleton in Richmond, Virginia.[14]

Nathan Boone: I don't recollect of Father going to Richmond to the legislature, except about 1790. I think he could not have gone in early 1780 when he went to buy warrants, as the object he then had in view was one of importance; and when robbed and defeated in the object, he turned and went home. If he went to Richmond as a legislator in the fall of 1780, then perhaps upon Arnold's invasion the legislature adjourned awhile to meet at Charlottesville. That would have been early the following May or June. Perhaps there may be something in this story, as Major Redd says my father and Ben Logan were Kentucky members whom he saw at Richmond in the latter part of 1780.

Draper: Logan's family says he was a member at Charlottesville when it was broken up by Tarleton.[15]

Nathan Boone: I have heard that when Jack Jouett gave notice of Tarleton's approach, my father and some others remained, loading up on wagons some of the public records, until some of the light horses entered the town.[16] My father and Jouett started off in a slow, unconcerned walk, when they were overtaken by the British, questioned hastily, and dismissed. Then Father, who had probably been first examined, walked on leisurely. But when Jouett was through, he called out, "Wait a minute, Captain Boone, and I'll go with you." Then said the British officer, "Ah, is he a captain?" and at the same time ordered him to stop and took him into custody.

Father was conveyed to the British camp and put into a coal house and kept all night. It was rainy, so he presented a dirty appearance the next morning. Then he was taken before Colonel Tarleton and examined, either then or the next day, but they released him. He very probably explained his title of captain by referring to his old Dunmore commission. My father also may have pretended contentment and sung songs while confined.

When Father returned home, he found he had during the previous March (the 2d) had a son born; and during his absence and also at the same station, two grandchildren, one by Mrs. Flanders Callaway and the other by Mrs. William Hays. All the children were nearly the same age. He was presented successively with the grandchildren, which he said were not his, but quickly recognized the right one, which was me!

Draper: Tell me of Holder's defeat and the death of Captain Nathaniel Hart in 1782.

Nathan Boone: I have heard Father tell of this, but I cannot recall any of the particulars, nor about his pursuing Indians who killed Captain Hart.[17]

6

Bryan's Station and the Blue Licks Defeat

Lyman Draper: I would assume that Colonel Boone told you about the relief of Bryan's Station and the Battle of Blue Licks.

Nathan Boone: Absolutely. William Hays, my brother-in-law, headed the party from Boone's Station that went to the relief of Bryan's Station. Hays was a brave man and always foremost, but he was bad-tempered and drank to excess. He was eventually killed by his son-in-law, about 1808 on the Femme Osage, in St. Charles County, Missouri.[1]

The men from Boone's Station somewhere joined the Lexington men and marched to Bryan's together. Prior to reaching the fort, there was a half-mile-long lane with fences on both sides. They had proceeded about halfway down this lane when the Indians were discovered behind the fence on both sides. William Hays and others jumped over the fence.[2] Hays was on horseback and received a bullet wound through the back of the neck, which so stunned him that he was insensible or nearly so for a short distance, but maintained his position on his horse and escaped.

My father raised a party of men from the vicinity of his station. William Hays was not with the company because of his wound. While marching from Bryan's to the Blue Licks, he became convinced that the Indians wished to be pursued, as they courted it by their signs. On the second morning the American force finally saw a few Indians leisurely retiring to the north across the Licking River. This led to a halt and the council of officers. My father mentioned that the Indians would ambush them at the head of the two ravines beyond the clearing where the timber began.[3] He first proposed to stop where they were or even fall back upon Benjamin Logan, who was following with additional troops. If they were determined to attack the enemy, he insisted they go either up or down the river beyond the peninsula and fall upon the enemy's rear.

My father was about to convince the other officers to follow his advice, when Hugh McGary spurred his horse into the water, calling out, "All who are not damned cowards follow me, and I'll soon show you the Indians." One after another began to follow under this imputation. Seeing the mass going, my father, who thought Major McGary was throwing out an imputation against his bravery, said, "I can go as far as any man," and took his place in front of the advancing soldiers, as did the other officers.[4]

The Kentucky troops crossed the river and rode on to within two hundred yards of where some Indians began to jump up and fall back a little, as if appearing to retreat. The men dismounted, hitched their horses, and fastened their surplus clothing, coats, and hunting shirts to their saddles. My father, commanding the left wing, entered spiritedly into the action and drove the enemy back fully one hundred yards, killing a large number. He felt elated with the success and prospect of victory.[5]

Father had no sword but was armed with a very long English fowling piece, which he seldom used. He took it with him on this occasion and loaded each shot with three or four rifle bullets and sixteen or eighteen buckshot. During the battle the enemy would jump and fall back a piece and take another tree or stump, and it was thus on one of the retreats that he killed an Indian and passed by his body during the attack. Though elated with the Indians retreating at that time, subsequently, when finding how the battle had gone, Father concluded the retreat was probably a feint on the part of the Indians to draw the Fayette militia under him into the trap. Not long after the fighting began, Major McGary came riding up, exclaiming: "Colonel Boone, why are you not retreating? Todd and Trigg's line has given way, and the Indians are all around you." Then my father ordered his men to collect together and in a body break through the enemy, for he found the Indians were already in his rear. Upon reaching the horses, each man took the first within his reach and each then shifted for himself.

My brother Israel Boone had been sick with the slow fever but was recovering, so Father kept near him, got him a horse, and told him to

Depiction of the Battle of Blue Licks, from *Adventures of Daniel Boone* by Henry J. Wehman. Courtesy of Missouri Historical Society, St. Louis.

mount and make his escape; then he himself ran for a horse. Israel, instead of having mounted and started off as Father expected, lingered to wait for Father. Father, amid the cracking of guns, heard some struggling on the ground and discovered Israel had fallen with blood gushing from his mouth, obviously a mortal wound. This was subsequently ascertained when burying the dead, as he discovered the wound was through or near his heart. Father had barely time to mount and escape, using the same horse (belonging to Mrs. Edward Boone) he had given to Israel. During the retreat Father wheeled off from the main route of the retreating men, left the trail, went to the right, and forded the river about half a mile below the main ford at the lick. He continued his retreat until he met Logan's party.

My father always thought what caused the retreat after the first fire must have been that Todd and Trigg were then killed, and the loss of their leaders dispirited the men. He used to speak of Benjamin Netherland stopping on horseback just south of the ford, halting a few men, and firing on the Indians. He said this enabled the fugitives to pass the ford.

My cousin Squire Boone, afterward designated as Preacher Squire Boone, had a thigh broken. His father was Samuel Boone, brother of my father. After the battle a young man [named Samuel Brannon] placed him on his, the young man's, horse. They went along and both rode over the Licking River. Brannon pushed off some other fugitives who jumped up on behind. Squire Boone did not cross at the main ford, as he had one of the high hills to climb. He rode home, which was probably then at Boone's Station, with the limb dangling. He had it dressed and got well, though splinters of bone came out for some years after. He and his father settled on Boone Creek, probably in Clark County. They lived about four miles east-southeast from Boone's Station. It was Samuel Brannon, a raw young man scarcely grown, who thus befriended Squire Boone, and my father used to speak highly of the act. He said that Brannon got killed when ascending the high hill over Licking.

The remark "You be there!" which Captain John Gass says Boone used when he killed the Indian at the Blue Licks battle must have related to the Indian he killed in the battle. My father used to say that he believed he had killed Indians on other occasions; he was only positive of having killed this one.

Father never censured the conduct of Colonels Todd and Trigg. He only said that if they were not killed or disabled at the first fire, which he believed was the case, they must have acted cowardly.

My father went with Logan's party to bury the dead.[6] He recognized his son Israel from the locality and some marks. My poor brother's face was blackened and swollen, as were all the others on the battle ground, but none of the bodies (which my father used to say was remarkable) were torn or eaten by varmints. Father used to be deeply affected, even to tears, when he spoke of the Blue Licks defeat and the death of his son.

Father used to say that from the returned prisoners taken at the Blue Licks it was learned that the Indians, upon counting their loss and numbering the scalps taken, found their loss exceeded the whites by four. They then had four of the prisoners killed to make the number even. He believed the Indians killed the four and gave this excuse for doing so, but he never believed that the Indian loss was so great.[7] The returned prisoners also said that the Indians remarked that if the whites in the battle had delivered one more fire, the Indians would have given way; but this Father did not believe. But had the center and right lines fought as well and successfully as his own, he would have thought there was some truth in this acknowledgment of the Indians.

Olive Boone: Colonel Boone used to say he knew every inch of ground around Blue Licks. He knew the Indians were in the ravines ready to ambush them, and that the whites would be whipped like dogs. It grieved him to think into what a hopeless engagement they were about to enter. However, Colonel Boone felt that McGary's imputation was mainly aimed at him, as he was the first to urge they wait for Logan and said he knew he could go where any of them could.

Daniel Boone used to quote Benjamin Netherland when in good conduct he formed up a few men south of the ford: "Let's halt, boys, and give them a fire." It had a happy effect in checking the Indians and permitting those at and near the ford to get off. He said that there was great slaughter at the ford.

Colonel Boone got the Widow Edward Boone's horse, which some of the Boone's Station men had ridden out, and gave it to Israel to mount and ride off. Israel said "Father, I won't leave you," and the colonel told him to make his escape, and he would find a horse. Colonel Boone went to get another, heard something, looked around as he was passing, for he was within a few yards of his son (who he supposed had gone), and saw him falling. The blood was gushing from his mouth several inches, and his arms were stretched out and shivering. Colonel Boone seized the same horse he had provided for his hapless son and rode off. A platoon shot near him and down fell a forked branch across his horse's neck, but he escaped. They found Israel had been shot through the heart when he came back later with the burial party.

Squire Boone, Colonel Boone's nephew, was three days reaching home with his broken thigh. Colonel Boone would shed tears when speaking of Israel's death and the sad events of that day. Israel had long been sick previously and had recovered or nearly so, leaving him with a stiff neck, and his father and family tried all they could to persuade him not to go, but he would go. Colonel Boone used to lament that Israel did go and that he did not ride off when he first gave him the horse.

Colonel Boone told me the prisoners killed by Indians to even the numbers were tomahawked.

Nathan Boone: I also recall some of the incidents on Clark's campaign in 1782. At one time there were several Indian prisoners placed in a cabin, and Hugh Leeper rushed in and tomahawked one of them, a fine-looking young warrior. He was much censured for it. At least this is as Father spoke of it. There was something about Leeper's making an apology, being that the Indian was his prisoner.

Father used to mention going to Willstown, as he called it, and finding the Indians had fled. The troops then plundered and burned it. He said that Logan's party reached Loramie's store in the night.[8] The trader, Loramie, heard them, blew out his candle, and dodged behind the door. When the store was filled with Clark's men, Loramie slipped through the crowd and escaped. Several Indian towns were destroyed on this campaign.

In the fall of 1784 we moved out of Boone's Station and settled his farm, a new place on Marble Creek, about five miles nearly west of Boone's Station. There was no forting there. We probably raised, at most, two crops in 1784 and 1785.[9] Father was justice and sheriff and deputy surveyor. When we moved, William Hays, my brother-in-law, came into possession of the Marble Creek place and remained there till the fall of 1799, when he moved in company with us to Missouri.[10]

Next we moved to Limestone, probably in early 1786.[11] Between Blue Licks and Limestone we traveled through the thick cane region, and several buffaloes ran from the thick cane across the road and knocked one of the packhorses over and scared several of the horses. The buffaloes when unhurt do not act this way, but they must have heard the noise or smelled the coming horse cavalcade and mistook its direction. They emerged from the thick cane and were upon the horses so suddenly as to knock over the horse in running across the trail and dodging into the cane on the opposite side. This incident was one of the earliest events treasured in my memory.

At Limestone my father kept a tavern, or house of entertainment, and also a warehouse for the storage of goods. He also worked as deputy surveyor.

Draper: Did Colonel Boone go out on Logan's campaign in 1786?[12]

Nathan Boone: Yes, he went out with Logan, and on arriving at the Indian town, the Indians fled. Some dogs were seen running, and Father said if they would follow these dogs they would find the Indians. He and his party pursued on horseback and soon discovered several Indians running off, and as they gained on them, one of the Indians was looking back over his shoulder. Father was mounted on a pony somewhat in the rear of the pursuers and recognized the Indian by his remarkable physiognomy. He called out to those with him: "Mind that fellow—I know him—it's Big Jim, who killed my son in Powell's Valley." Two or three dismounted, and Big Jim, apparently hearing what Father said, whirled about and fired at one of the men on horseback, who fell off dead.[13] Big Jim almost at the same moment fell wounded in the tall grass. While the white men were gathering around the dead man who had fallen from his horse, Big Jim reloaded his gun, and as some of the men approached him, he killed or wounded another. Then some of the men rushed up and shot him.

Draper: I have seen some notes that show your father was one of the negotiators during the Limestone Treaty, when Indian prisoners were traded for white prisoners.

Nathan Boone: Father carried on the treaty in 1787, and I think, from my faint recollection, that the Indians camped on the flat just above the mouth of Limestone Creek, where there were then trees standing.

A couple of young Indians were left as hostages for the bringing in of other prisoners, who were kept in custody by my father. They were finally released, and for their protection my father sent his son, my brother Daniel, to go with them a few miles beyond the Ohio into the wilderness. They seemed to discover that my brother appeared somewhat suspicious of them, and they told him he might return, so he got home the same evening.

My father's warehouse at Limestone was located just below the mouth of Limestone Creek and near the riverbank. Our residence was a few yards lower down and farther back from the water. During the fall and winter of 1787 and winter following, Father was busily employed in digging ginseng. He employed several hands for this work and also bought up what he could. We were old enough to camp out among the hills to help with the digging. By the next spring we had some twelve or fifteen tons, which we loaded into a keelboat, and Father started up the river with his family with him, destined for Philadelphia to the market.

Father left his son-in-law Philip Goe to operate his warehouse and run the business at Limestone. At the head of the large island just above Gallipolis, the only island between Gallipolis and Point Pleasant, we attempted to cross, but with the strong current at the head of the island, the boat careened upon the driftwood at the head of the island and filled with water in the shallow water. No lives were lost, but everything in the boat got wet, and the ginseng was damaged. We sent to Point Pleasant for help to raise the boat. It was only three miles away.

John Van Bibber and others came to Father's aid. We dried some of the ginseng spread on shore, but all was injured, so Father didn't get half the regular price. The delay at Point Pleasant caused him to reach Philadelphia just after a fall in the price. As it was, Father lost money by the operation. All of the roots had to be washed when dug, then strung and dried in the sun.

By John Van Bibber's invitation, our family stopped a while at his house, while Father was getting the boat and cargo ready to resume the trip. At Van Bibber's we left a little white girl whom Father had brought up from Limestone. She had been released from captivity by the Indians at the treaty in 1787 and had since lived with our family. Her name was Chloe Flinn; she was ten years old and had been taken prisoner from Greenbriar in Virginia. She was subsequently sent back there to her friends.

This John Van Bibber was my wife's uncle. He had settled in Greenbriar, from the Yadkin, before the Revolution. He lived there in 1774 and was in the Point Pleasant battle. With several others, Ferguson and Bronson among them, Van Bibber made a very successful bear hunt in the fall.[14] They made canoes, partly filled them with the bear oil, and started for Natchez to the market, a place used greatly by Spaniards and French in various cookeries. Before reaching there they unfortunately concluded to practice a deception by pouring in a quantity of water in the canoes, so that the oil would rise on top. They sold the whole cargo by estimating the amount. They had not got far from Natchez, returning by land, when they were overtaken by a superior party in pursuit.

They were fired on and some killed; the survivors dispersed, and some starved.

My father went out on a hunting tour in about January or early February of 1780.[15] The winter before he was in Carolina, and the [next] winter he was mostly if not entirely in Virginia serving in the legislature. He was away when I was born, on March 2, 1781. While hunting he came across the tracks of a man in the snow, followed them a little distance, and overtook him. It proved to be John Van Bibber, in a nearly starving condition and without ammunition. He related his adventure and hardships and said that his companion Bronson had given out a mile or so behind from weakness and exhaustion, where he had stopped to die. They soon reached Bronson, and they all went to Father's hunting camp. There they soon recovered. As Van Bibber had a gun, Father furnished them with ammunition, and they went on home.

Ferguson, a neighbor of Van Bibber's and another of the bear oil party, also got home. Several were understood to have perished, which is probably evidence it happened during the hard winter of 1779-1780. Killing bear when fattened on the fall mast would probably have taken some twenty-five days, and going down to Natchez in canoes and good water would have given about the proper time for slow traveling in snow to reach Kentucky in January or February. But I think this bear oil trip could not have been so early and doubt whether at that period it would have been known in Greenbriar that the oil was marketable in Natchez.

My father had heard nothing from John Van Bibber from this time until Van Bibber helped him with the ginseng at Point Pleasant. Two daughters living with Mrs. John Van Bibber were Mrs. Colonel Andrew Donnally and Mrs. John Reynolds. Both lived at or near Kanawha saltworks. John Van Bibber was in the Point Pleasant battle and at that time lived on Greenbriar.

After the wreck near Point Pleasant, in a week or so we resumed our trip up the Ohio. Without any further accident we reached Redstone in cherry time. There his daughter, my sister Mrs. Goe, resided. We stopped and stayed with her husband's parents until her father returned.

There the gingseng was packed on horses and transported to Colonel Thomas Hart in Hagerstown, Maryland. We made but a short stay in Philadelphia and then went to Father's old neighborhood in Berks County. The family members on this trip were my parents, myself, and

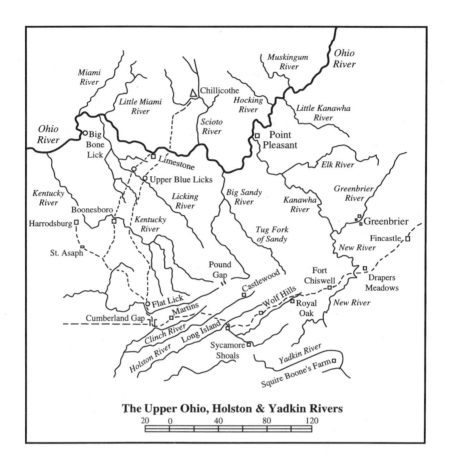

The Upper Ohio, Holston & Yadkin Rivers

two brothers. This visit was in the fall and winter of 1788-1789. We returned by sleigh to Redstone, perhaps by way of Hagerstown, for on behalf of Colonel Hart, there Father purchased a stock of goods for the frontier trade. Then he also decided to take up residence at Point Pleasant and not return to Maysville as he had originally intended when he left there.

Draper: Colonel Daniel Boone passed Fort Harmar in May 1789, as Colonel Harmar's diary shows.

Nathan Boone: I believe we went on down to Maysville, as I well recollect I was there and witnessed with my own eyes the dragging of

Lewis Wetzel down the riverbank at Maysville. A party of soldiers dragged him by his long hair, tied or cued, and this was in the daytime.[16] I also saw Lewis Wetzel at Point Pleasant, probably after this occurrence.

Olive Boone: I also recollect seeing him there. His exploits were quite notorious. About 1804, we heard James Morrison, of Missouri, since deceased, who said that some years previous he was down the river to New Orleans and thence by sea to Philadelphia, and Lewis Wetzel was on board. Off the Florida reefs in some gale, he got thrown off into the sea, probably in the night. There he remained several hours but was picked up and saved. Previously to this, Lewis had been living with some family near Natchez, and he gave some counterfeit coin to the children and was put in the calaboose. He was kept there a good while but finally was liberated. He married a French woman of some property. Afterward he went with Morrison by sea to Philadelphia. This was the last either Morrison or I knew of Wetzel. Colonel Daniel Boone knew him well, probably first on Logan's campaign. The military apprehension of Wetzel at Limestone or Maysville caused much excitement there.

Colonel Boone bought up a drove of horses in Kentucky during this visit and sent them to Colonel Hart at Hagerstown in custody of his sons Daniel and Jesse. They were driven by a new land route across the Sandy River. During the long drive, horses escaped, and Colonel Boone was not able to earn enough from them to cover their cost. The proceeds were applied in liquidating the balance due on his stock of merchandise.[17]

7

POINT PLEASANT

Nathan Boone: After he settled and closed his business at Limestone, my father, Daniel Boone, gathered up his movable property and there sold out his merchandise. He then moved and began residing at Point Pleasant in one of the upper occupied houses just up the Kanawha from the Point. He did not renew the stock of merchandise except probably once and possibly not at all. He had to trade for furs and peltries.

Lyman Draper: I have a document which shows that in October 1789, Daniel Boone was recommended to the governor by the court of Mason County, Virginia, for the commission of lieutenant colonel and that he was qualified for this commission on April 4, 1791. He also represented the county in the Virginia legislature. But please continue and tell me about the time Jacob Van Bibber was taken.

Nathan Boone: This was in October 1789. Matthias Van Bibber, my wife's brother, the son of Peter Van Bibber [Jr.], who was in the Point Pleasant battle, was young but a grown man. He had two brothers, John and Isaac, and the latter was also killed. Peter Van Bibber died at Point Pleasant on October 10, 1796, at about age sixty-three; John lived for several years after Jesse Boone moved to Missouri.

The men went out hunting in the latter part of October 1789 and killed a bear about three miles above Point Pleasant but a distance back from the river. [Matthias] returned home and the next morning took a horse to pack in the meat and took with him his younger brother Jacob, born in the spring of 1775 and now fourteen years old. They loaded the meat, and Jacob mounted on the horse, and with Matthias on foot they had proceeded but a short distance, about half a mile, when they were fired upon by one of a party of three Indians. (Perhaps it would be more accurate to say two Indians and one white man.) They were Shawnees who had been hiding in a treetop only some ten paces off.

Matthias Van Bibber received a flesh wound in the head above the eye and fell stunned but quickly recovered and escaped. The white Indian of the party seized Jacob and the horse, and a portion of the meat was taken by the Indians, and two dogs the boys had with them followed Jacob and the horse. The Indians soon crossed the Ohio and were beyond reach.

It was while Jacob was a prisoner that the affair of [John] May's boat occurred.[1] I heard this from the surviving girl, Peggy Fleming. Both sisters lived with their parents for several years at Point Pleasant. They were very handsome girls but of bad repute, and during the summer I heard the story again through Mrs. Tacket. They said the Indians had taken Jacob on this very trip when May's boat was attacked, and he was to have been used as the decoy. However, his Indian sister had cut her foot, and Jacob was left to take care of her. They remained at the Indian encampment a mile or two from the river; but after the affair he was taken to the scene of the defeat to aid in packing in the plunder. There he saw Dolly Fleming's body and instantly recognized it. It lay upon the treetop at the water's edge. At the time he did not know the names of the others, but when they took the first load of plunder to camp, there he found Peggy Fleming, [Jacob] Skyles, and [William] Flinn. In September 1790, being sent out to hunt horses, he got lost and decided to make his way for the settlements. He reached the Ohio River the seventh day, including two days he spent trying to find Indians. He had nothing to eat except for some young butternuts. He steered his course by using the moss on the north side of the trees. He crossed the river about a mile below Belleville, [Ohio], and reached home after eleven months' captivity.

Mr. Skyles, if it was Skyles instead of Flinn who was burned, had received a wound across his back, which the Indians cured. Then a squaw told Skyles that the Indians intended to burn him and advised him to run away; he did not believe it, and he would not go without Peggy Fleming, whom he hoped to marry. He was burned, and young Van Bibber was within hearing distance of the cries of the poor man. At least as a prisoner he did not have to witness such a spectacle.

Peggy subsequently returned to Point Pleasant. She joined the troops of either General St. Clair or General Wayne [as a camp follower] and went off. I heard no more of her. She and her sister had previously been army women at Pittsburgh. From there they moved to Point Pleasant, as it was more beautiful.

When Jacob Van Bibber reached the Ohio, he saw a canoe ascending to Belleville with two men and two women in it. One man, named Scott, was a tailor who had worked at Point Pleasant. He called to them to come and get him. They asked who he was. He said a prisoner from the Indians. They said they reckoned he was a prisoner from hell and had a hundred Indians to welcome them if they were to go after him. He told his name and his parents', who were acquaintances at Point Pleasant whom Scott knew. Scott also knew that Van Bibber had been taken and finally went timidly, with the women crying. They gave him an apple and took him to Belleville. He ate some bread and milk at Belleville but little more. He was cautious about eating. That evening he started for home in a canoe with a little bread and meat and arrived at Point Pleasant the next evening. He was not very hungry till the third day after reaching Belleville. During his capture his Indian brother once told him that he was to be burned, which caused him to go to his mother crying. She punished her son for saying so and said that she never would permit her own adopted son to be burned. Not long ago Jacob Van Bibber was living near Greenupsburg, Kentucky.[2]

Draper: What do you remember about your father serving in the legislature?

Nathan Boone: I think it was in the fall of 1789 that my father went to Richmond, as he had just settled at the Point. There were but two or three settlements in the country with small populations, and with Father being engaged in trade he would soon have made the acquaintance of all the principal people. Besides, his Kentucky fame must have preceded him to Point Pleasant. But perhaps it was in the fall of 1790 when Father went to Richmond, or it may have been in the fall of 1791 or 1792. But not later.

In the fall of 1793 I was in Kentucky at school, and Father was certainly elected to office before I went there to school.[3] My mother and I went to Richmond with him, leaving my brothers Daniel and Jesse in

Point Pleasant to manage his business. I well recall that it was in the fall of the year when Father was in the legislature. I can remember gathering persimmons in my hat and nearly ruining it. I went to the statehouse and got the doorkeeper to go and call Father, getting pocket money from him to buy small things. Among others I remember getting oysters in the shell down at the river and roasting them in the shells at fires on the beach; the weather was cold, and we would shiver and hover up around the fire. On the return home (I think it was in winter or very early in spring) we visited Henry Miller in Augusta County, Virginia. There my father saw among Miller's cattle an animal of unusually large horns; he expressed a wish that he had one of them, as it would make a splendid powder horn. Miller said he planned to kill the cow in a few days and would do it now and did so. He gave Father the desired horn and he engraved his name and the year upon it. My father eventually lost it on one of his early hunting trips in Missouri by the Indians getting it.[4]

In the summer of 1790, just a few days before he was married, Jesse B. Boone started for the mouth of Elk River, now Charleston, where the county seat was located. He went for a marriage license. Those were dangerous times, so he was accompanied by James and Matthias Van Bibber, brothers, and their cousin Isaac Van Bibber (who later married Elizabeth Hays, the granddaughter of my father, Colonel Daniel Boone). Also in the party were William Craig and two young men both with the name of William Hall, but they were in no way related. They went up the river in a canoe.

When within a few miles of the Coal Fort, located at the mouth of Coal River or perhaps a short distance above the mouth,[5] they discovered a person on shore in the woods. By his dress and actions they thought he was an Indian. They landed and slipped up on him, and Isaac Van Bibber was about to shoot him when someone yelled he was a white man. Van Bibber lowered his gun. They were so close that he couldn't escape without exposing himself to certain death. They took him prisoner. He said his name was England, that he had a hunting companion named Ireland, who was in the woods hunting! He could give no satisfactory account of himself and had a strange, suspicious appearance. Finally he managed to escape from them, much to the regret of the party. They fully believed that he was one of the Indian party who a few days afterwards attacked and took Coal Fort, and they really wished they had killed him.

On their return Jesse Boone's party tarried overnight at Coal Fort, and the young men went out into the watermelon patch to eat melons in a field adjoining the fort, partly cultivated and partly in log heaps. Later they learned that the Indians were hiding in the field behind the patch and in the log heaps at that time. The Indian party was probably not large. They had seen Boone's armed party go to the fort and would not attack while they were there. Boone's party soon departed and safely reached Point Pleasant, but an hour or so later Coal Fort was attacked.

A man named David Robinson, who had formerly lived there, visited Coal Fort with his wife to get some flax they had left there, and that night Robinson had a bad dream which caused him to jump out of bed. He had a bad dream about his children left at home, and he told his wife they would let the flax go and return home. His wife teased him and said he acted like an old crazy woman. But they left and were yet within hearing when the attack was made.

At the very moment of the attack, a man in the part of the fort nearest the river, being farthest from the attack, seized his sick wife and young child, bore them hastily to a canoe, and escaped. The fort was soon overrun, as perhaps there was no resistance. Several were killed, including a young man named Samuel Tackett. The fort and the dead burned together. Mrs. Tacket, her son Lewis, and her daughter Elizabeth, both grown, were among the captives. They subsequently returned, and my wife saw them, together with another woman who was also a returned captive. At the time, old Mr. Tacket, with some of his children, was absent, having gone to the old settlements in Virginia.

In the summer of 1791 or perhaps 1792, Joseph Burrell and Andrew Lewis, who were either nephews or cousins of Colonel Thomas Lewis of Point Pleasant, started in a canoe from Elk River. They carried an express to Point Pleasant. In the morning they were near Twenty-Five Mile Creek and discovered some canoes fastened to shore loaded with corn and bacon. These some Indians had stolen and now had landed to waylay someone. Lewis insisted on going to see, but Burrell opposed the idea. They finally went over to the canoes, and when sufficiently near, both were shot and wounded. Burrell was shot through the body near the hips, and Lewis had an arm broken and was thrown out into the river; he was standing up paddling. Burrell helped him back into the canoe and, disabled as he was, managed to paddle, while Lewis cursed the Indians while near enough to make them hear. When they reached Point Pleasant, they had to send to Gallipolis for two doctors to amputate Lewis's arm. This happened after the first settlement of Gallipolis, which I think was early in 1791.

My father became a lieutenant colonel in the militia about 1791, but there was some dispute between him and Colonel Andrew Donnally Sr. relative to the rank, but Father gained the point of difference. Father may not have been county lieutenant at this time, particularly if the county was organized in 1789.

Two or three companies of militia were sent from Greenbriar for the protection of the Point Pleasant frontier, and my father assigned them their regions of defense. He sent the company of Captain Moses Mann up to Belleville. The captain had two brothers in his company, Thomas and William Mann. While stationed at Belleville they started for a neighboring lick to deer hunt. They passed Mrs. Mary Galrooth washing clothes in the river; they splashed her; she splashed them. They ended by ducking her and holding her head under water so long she nearly drowned. Recovering herself, she told them in her plain Scotch as they were going off that "she hoped to God the Indians might kill them, and they never return." The Indians attacked them shortly thereafter and both were killed. This happened in 1791 or 1792, when Father qualified as colonel and before I went to Kentucky to school.

Draper: What can you tell me about Ben Eulan's Leap?

Nathan Boone: This was before 1792, before Joseph Van Bibber was taken, and while I was still at Point Pleasant. Ben Eulan went out hunting on the hills about three-fourths of a mile below the mouth of the Kanawha. He saw some Indians, perhaps four or five of them, who chased him. He was not thinking where he was going and found himself going at full speed on the edge of the Ohio cliffs. He then threw his rifle to the ground, jumped down and into the top of a standing buckeye, sixty-three feet, and thus through it, eased his fall. The limbs of a buckeye run up like the pine and are soft and brittle. In falling he broke off several limbs, which were two or three inches in size, and bent others. He landed upon his feet. He found himself on a ledge and then made another leap down to another ledge and then a third jump to the bottom. One of these leaps was eighteen feet; the other distance I have forgotten. Each time he landed upon his feet. After going but a short distance he became very sick and vomited up blood. He then lay down behind a log, as he thought he would die.[6]

He had broken some of the small internal blood vessels. But he soon recovered a little, made his way to the Kanawha River, and crossed. He came to Peter Van Bibber's, one of the nearest houses after crossing the river. Mr. Van Bibber was the only person in town who bled people, and he bled him in the forehead, both arms, and both feet. Though no bones were broken, he was much bruised and his system shocked. But he soon recovered. He had formerly been an Indian trader and had in some way displeased the Indians and had to leave them. He had reason to think they would put him to death if they ever got him, which gave him his motive for his leap.

Olive Boone: I heard him say the Indians had threatened to burn him. He was always afraid of being captured. The man kept a small store at Point Pleasant. At the time he seemed to be about twenty-five years of age, small and light, and weighed about a hundred pounds. Later he settled near Greenupburg, became a small farmer, and died there about 1816 or 1817, a year or so before Jesse Boone moved from there to Missouri in 1818. I don't know about his children except one of his sons was a preacher. He had three or more sons, one named John, and two daughters.

Nathan Boone: The smallpox was at Gallipolis, where they had it the latter part of the year, and the next spring it arrived at Point Pleasant. Jesse Boone's firstborn child died of it when only a few weeks old; this child was born January 9, 1793.

John Van Bibber, my wife's uncle, was afraid of the smallpox and retired to a cabin he owned opposite Point Pleasant in a large bottom. He had made small improvements there and used the place for making maple sugar. At that time he stayed there nearly all winter with his Negro man, David. In the spring his sixteen-year-old daughter, Rhoda, and her cousin, Joseph Van Bibber, crossed the river in a canoe from the Point. (Joseph was the brother of my wife. He was born in 1780 or 1781, so she was two years younger, having been born in January of 1783.)

Both Rhoda and Joseph had recovered from smallpox and were now thoroughly "cleaned up." Rhoda was preparing dinner, Joseph was picking up chips and sticks for the fire, and David was at work in the clearing about fifty to a hundred yards from the house. Mr. Van Bibber was sitting on a log reading between David and the house. Indians appeared, and David ran for the cabin "hallooing" as he ran. Mr. Van Bibber ran for the cabin and ordered his daughter and Joseph into the cabin. Either they didn't understand or thought the canoe safer, and ran for the river. Mr. Van Bibber and David got into the cabin and fastened the door. There were twelve to twenty Indians, divided into two groups. Some remained at the cabin, and the others followed Rhoda and Joseph, who had by then got the canoe out onto the water. The Indians fired at them and shot Rhoda through the body under the arms, killing her instantly. The Indians threatened to shoot Joseph, so he returned to shore. The Indians took Rhoda's scalp and led Joseph up the bank. He broke away but ran only about a hundred yards before he was retaken.

In the meantime the whole population of Point Pleasant lined the shore and witnessed the scene. All the men seized their guns and started over the river for the Indians, hoping to check the Indians and save the two in the canoe. I was among the rescuers with my small rifle. My father and the others fired about one hundred shots across the river, which was five hundred yards wide.

The Indians attacking the cabin were held off by John Van Bibber and David, who wounded three of them including White Loon, who had his arm broken. As soon as the people at Point Pleasant could get a large pirogue in the water, some fifteen or twenty jumped in with their rifles loaded and started over the river. Jesse Boone and Jacob Van Bibber were in this boat. The Indians retreated by the time the boat reached midstream.

Afterwards the Negro David was given a dead Indian's gun and silver bands and broaches. Afterwards he cut up the Indian's body. David was a short, heavy, and very muscular man. He could with apparent ease lift a barrel of whiskey by the chimes and raise it up and drink, standing, out of the bung. For his service that day against the Indians, Van Bibber gave him his freedom. He lived to an old age and died at Tay's Valley a few miles south of Point Pleasant.

Some of the Indians were Shawnee, and they took Joseph back to their village. He was, strangely enough, adopted into the same family who had formerly adopted his brother Jacob. Sometime in 1794 his Indian family went to Detroit to sell their furs and peltry. There Joseph escaped from them; he was aided by a Mr. Forsythe, who hid him in his house until the Indians stopped searching for him and went away. Forsythe went to the River Frenche, and Joseph went along, having hired out to work for him.[7]

His brother, Matthias Van Bibber, went to General Wayne's Treaty [at Greenville] in the summer of 1795 in hopes of finding and freeing him. But he was not there, so he went to Detroit, where the Indians said they had lost him. At Detroit he learned of his whereabouts and went and got him.

Returning through the woods in what is now Ohio, they met with a Miss Betsey Waggoner and her friends, who had freed her from captivity. She alone was mounted on horseback. Matthias became sick with fever, and Miss Waggoner gave up her horse for him to ride. During this trip of fourteen days, they had only boiled acorns to eat and one turkey that they killed. They reached the Ohio near the mouth of Big Beaver Creek and were nearly starved. They saw a boat coming down the Ohio, and Matthias recognized the voice of Jesse Boone, who took the Van Bibbers on board; the others were going up the river. Joseph Van Bibber died at Point Pleasant in September 1796.

In the summer of 1791 some men working the fields were attacked.[8] John Craig, Andrew Fleming, Jesse Boone, Thomas Hannon, James Van Bibber, Morris Reynolds, Jacob Van Bibber, and a large number of others were at work (generally some twenty to thirty at a time) in the common field of some 40 acres, situated about a quarter of a mile above the upper end of the town and about six hundred yards above the fort with a small piece of woods intervening. This field was parceled out to the citizens, and while working several would stand guard. Sometimes the Indians would waylay the field early in the morning when they came to work or at noon when they had gone home to dinner. On this occasion a party of about twenty or thirty Indians attacked the whites as they returned from dinner. The Indians waylaid them at the gap on the side next to the fort. They concealed themselves inside the fence in the weeds with their guns poking through the rails. They fired a whole volley at a distance not over ten paces away, but strange to say, none were injured by the fire.

The white men ducked behind trees and stood their ground. Reinforcements came out from the fort, so the Indians went off with their wounded. In the fighting, John Craig was mortally wounded and died ten hours later. Andrew Fleming was wounded in the arm. My father, Daniel Boone, dressed and attended his wound until he recovered.

Olive Boone: Colonel Boone generally attended to all gunshot cases, as he had more experience.

Nathan Boone: Jesse Boone took part in this fight. James Van Bibber, the son of John, fell at the first fire while he was running over the ploughed ground. An Indian tried to tomahawk him, but his cousin, James Van Bibber, the son of Peter, and Morris Reynolds shot this Indian. His companions carried him off.

Michael See and Robert Sinclair were killed in a similar attack in the summer of 1792. Jesse B. Boone and his father-in-law, Captain John Van Bibber, were in this affair. A Negro boy and a thirteen-year-old white boy named Hampton Northrop were captured. Jesse Boone found the body of a Dutchman, Joe Darr, in a brush heap, but Darr was only hiding, not dead.

John Bruce was killed about 1789 in the common field, but the Widow Lockhart and a Negro named Pompey, who belonged to Colonel Thomas Lewis, escaped to the fort. This affair was still being talked about when we moved to Point Pleasant.

My father, Daniel Boone, was chased by Indians in the fall of 1792[9] He and his son Daniel M[organ] were camped about a mile from the river on the first creek below Chickamauga Creek, which is the first below Gallipolis.[10] They were out deer hunting and became separated. Daniel M. Boone met three Indians, and two of them fired at him and missed. They chased him a half a mile or so, but being fleet on foot, he changed his course, lost them, and went to camp. My father was at camp; he heard the firing, so he concealed himself some little distance off to watch the camp. He soon had his fears relieved by his son's appearance. He gathered up their things and crossed to the southern side of the Ohio and returned home. He brought back a few deer skins and a little meat after the two-day hunt but decided hunting north of the Ohio was too dangerous.

The same fall, in 1792, my brother Daniel, William Hall, and

Matthias and Isaac Van Bibber, cousins, were out hunting and camped near the mouth of the same creek just described.[11] The first night they discovered Indians lurking about the camp. They took their things down to the river to load the canoe. They were delayed trying to get Matthias Van Bibber's dog into the boat, so he got out of the boat to catch the dog, but as he jumped on shore, an Indian stepped from behind the bushes. They were within a few yards of each other. The Indian and Van Bibber both uttered a "waugh" and Van Bibber jumped into the boat without the dog, and they got off without any further delays.

In April of 1793 my father was reported killed. I don't remember anything which could have given rise to this story. Perhaps I had then gone to Kentucky to school.

Olive Boone: I recollect that about this period Colonel Daniel Boone was out in the woods hunting; he overstayed his time, and as the Indians were very troublesome, great apprehensions were entertained for his safety, but he returned in safety.

Nathan Boone: About the fall of 1791, after the legislature adjourned, my father went buffalo hunting alone up the Kanawha [River] and camped near the mouth of Eighteen Mile Creek. In the river bottom he killed two buffaloes, more than he killed at any other time in the Kanawha country. On the other hunts he had only killed one or two animals. The buffalo were killed for the meat; deer, beaver, and bear for skins and fur for sale. He came home and took canoes, and together with myself and two or three other youths, he went back for the meat. He had it cut up and swung up on scaffolds. In going and returning I saw great numbers of possums coming down to the water's edge to drink. They were very fat from eating grapes and papaws, so I killed some and took them home to render up for their oil.

Sometime in 1793 I went to Kentucky.[12] There I stayed with Flanders Callaway and sometimes with William Hays, in Fayette county. Callaway resided on a branch of Hickman's Creek, about six miles from Boone's Station. I attended a school there, kept by Reverend John Rice, a Baptist clergyman. The school was about halfway between the residences of the Callaways and Hayses, who lived about two miles apart. There I remained till the latter part of 1794. When I left Kentucky I was accompanied on my trip by my brother Daniel, Matthias and Isaac Van

Bibber, and John Scholl. All four had been visiting friends in Kentucky or the Van Bibbers in Powell's Valley. We went to Maysville on foot and horseback, tying and riding. From there we took a canoe and went up the Ohio River to Point Pleasant. This was possibly in the fall, as the nights were cool.

In 1793 my father was at Paris, Kentucky, I think, to establish some land claims for a friend at Point Pleasant.

In the fall of 1794 Father and I were out hunting. We camped on the northern bank of the Ohio River, some two or three miles above the mouth of Campaign Creek, which was ten or twelve miles above Point Pleasant. It was frosty weather and leaves were falling. About the second morning, a foggy morning, my father went off, leaving me alone at camp. A large, fine buck came within twenty or twenty-five steps of camp. I seized my small rifle; this was not my little bird rifle which used a ball about the size of a buckshot. That one I used to kill birds and squirrels near Crooked Creek back of Point Pleasant. This larger rifle was made by my father and William Arbuckle, a gunsmith. I rested his gun against one of the camp posts and fired, but the deer ran off.

Father heard the shot and returned to camp. He asked me to point out where the deer had stood. There he found hair which the ball had cut off. He then followed the trail, found blood, and sixty or eighty yards further he found the deer dead. This was the first deer I ever killed.

But my father didn't leave me at camp anymore. He took me with him and two or three times pointed out deer, then showed me how to manage to get off shots. I was not to move or attempt to steal up on the deer when his head was up chewing and he was looking around, but to do so when his head was down feeding and could not so well see me. Following this advice, I killed one or two other deer during this hunt. While we were together, my father shot a bear, and one or two others when he was alone the first day. From these two or three bear we saved all the meat, and of the ten or fifteen deer we saved the best hindquarters.

On the fifth night, about midnight, I had been asleep for some time. But my father, Daniel Boone, heard a chopping or hacking some distance above and across the river. He awakened me and told me he thought the noise was made by Indians, as he thought it was made by their hatchets. He concluded that Indians had probably seen the fire at our camp and were making a raft to cross. We carried meat and skins to our canoe, which was twenty-five yards from camp, and returned to our fire again. The night was clear and frosty and a little foggy, so we remained at our fire with our blankets for some little time. After the chopping ceased we then went to our canoe; there we stayed some ten minutes until we heard the Indians paddling in the water. At that time we pushed off, and Father ordered me to roll his blanket around myself and lie down in the canoe. He sat in the stern, put the paddle carefully in the water, and then gave a push. We went forward noiselessly and were soon in the main current, which washed us down the river.

On the way Father put his head over the canoe and close to the water and said he thought he could catch a glimpse of the Indians. He had looked between the surface of the water and the fog, which did not quite reach to the water. Soon we were beyond harm. We reached Point Pleasant by daylight and learned that Daniel M. Boone and Matthias Van Bibber had each lost a horse that night. Daniel M. Boone raised a small party of men and pursued them but found the Indians had made their raft and crossed the river, as my father had supposed. They discovered evidence that the Indians had divided into two groups; one had left with the stolen horses, and the other had gone across the river to attack our camp.

Nearly the entire time I lived at Point Pleasant there were Indian troubles. The Indians would frequently get upon the high ridge behind the town, just above Crooked Creek. There they would erect blinds and spy out what they could discover. The fort was some 250 yards above the Point, not at the site of Lewis's old fort, which was on the Ohio.[13] The old fort covered about half an acre and was nearly square. Our fort was picketed or stockaded between the houses. The people in the area would flee at every alarm or dangerous period to this fort.

Captain John Van Bibber lived adjoining the fort on the south or lower side. This house was connected with another building, a blockhouse with the upper part projecting. Our family would stay in the second story of this blockhouse during these alarms. Captain Van Bibber would remain in his house, and all other families would leave their dwellings in town and take refuge in the fort. This fleeing to the fort occurred almost every year and sometimes several times a year. When our spies discovered that the Indians had left the country, the people would return to their houses. We usually stayed in the fort a week or ten days.

About the summer of 1792 a large body of Indians camped on Chiccaumauga [*sic*] Creek with the obvious intention of attacking either Gallipolis or Point Pleasant or both. They remained a week or ten days or more. The Point Pleasant spies reported that the Indians numbered four or five hundred. While the spies watched the Indians, the principal men of Gallopolis and Point Pleasant, consisting of my father, Daniel Boone, Colonel Lewis, and Captain Van Bibber, met to decide whether with their combined forces they were numerous enough to attack the Indians. They found they were not unless they left both places defenseless. The Indians did some minor mischief, then moved on. Our spies were Isaac Van Bibber and Vach Dickerson. Matthias Van Bibber also served as a spy for a while after being appointed by Colonel Bogue.[14]

8

BACK TO KENTUCKY

Nathan Boone: While at school in Kentucky, I formed an attachment for the place, and more especially for the quietness and safety of the interior from Indian dangers. I wanted my parents to move back to Kentucky, and they agreed.

In the spring or summer of 1795, I came down the Ohio with my father and mother. We landed at Limestone and proceeded to Bourbon County, where we settled on a tract of unimproved land owned by my brother Daniel M. Boone. The little farm was on the waters of the Brushy Fork of Hinkston, about six miles east of Millersburg. We lived on land in the fork between Brushy Fork and Hinkston Creek in what is now Nicholas County. We were about twelve miles from the Lower Blue Licks.[1]

Our spring ran into Brushy Fork. We brought along provisions needed for the first year. My father and I killed a few deer, and we lived mostly on venison. We cleared ten acres and raised two crops there, in 1796 and 1797. We spent the first fall and winter preparing for the crops. In the fall of 1796, my father and I, along with his son-in-law Flanders Callaway and two persons named Maupin and White, started for a fall and winter's bear hunt. We each took a horse, but we had no traps. In traveling to the settlement on the Big Sandy River, we killed but a single bear. On the way we passed the Burning Springs and then went on to the Big Sandy River, probably near the present Prestonsburg. We did not go far above where we first reached the river, and we certainly did not go up to what are now called the Louisa and Russell Forks.

On this hunt, Maupin and White were so discouraged, they soon returned to the settlements. They left just beyond the Burning Springs.

There was a settlement at Young's saltworks, with three or four families and a few work hands, and another small settlement of three or four families about four miles below. We reached the river at the lower settlement where we halted for a few days. Here we were told that there were some bear on a creek about nine miles down the river and on the east side. We went there and named it Greasy Creek; there we camped and killed some thirty or forty bears by New Year's, when the bears went into hibernation.[2]

A man came into the settlement with a horse load of bear meat. He didn't want to tell us where the bear were shot, but my father said he could follow his tracks anyway, so the man directed him to Greasy Creek. We saved the skins and smoked the meat. When spring came we made a canoe, and the men took the load of meat down the river. My father and I returned by land with the horses. The bear meat was unloaded at Limestone and carried to Bourbon County. Here we found the bear meat would bring more when rendered into oil; the oil brought a dollar a gallon and a bear's carcass would yield from ten to twenty gallons.

The next fall, in 1797, for some reason my father did not go out to hunt, but my brother Jesse and I and Flanders Callaway went up Sandy River for another bear hunt. That year Jesse had moved down and settled on the same tract with us. We went to the same region as the previous year. Major Andrew Hood was by then living at the lower settlement on Sandy [River], and we had a very successful hunt.[3] We killed 156 bears, which were smoked and floated down the river at the beginning of spring. Likewise, this bear meat was rendered into oil and used chiefly by the tanners. We waggoned the meat from Limestone to Grassy Fork.[4] Bear skins were then worth and sold for about two dollars, but sometimes they reached as high as four or five dollars.

In the spring of 1798 I started for the mouth of Little Sandy River with Jonathan Bryan. (He was the son of James and a brother of Joseph Bryan, the father-in-law of my father, Daniel Boone.) We planned to open an unimproved tract of land owned by my family, which was located about half a mile above the mouth of Little Sandy, on the southern bank of the Ohio. When we got there we found it pretty heavily timbered, so they decided to raise our first crop upon a nearby unoccupied tract which would be easier to clear. So we went up the Ohio River about ten miles and found a rich bottom with a small growth of timber and began preparing for a crop. This clearing, because of the numerous grapevines tangled in the tops of the small trees, proved to be much more laborious than we had expected. However, we finally got in eight acres of corn and raised a fair crop.

During the spring, I decided to take a couple of traps and go over to Blaine Creek and catch some beaver where I had seen some beaver signs.[5] I went alone on horseback with four or five of my dogs. I traveled up the east fork of Little Sandy River a little way above the fork, where I unexpectedly met six or eight buffaloes. My dogs chased one and had him flat upon his side. Instead of shooting the buffalo, I took my knife and went up to stab it, but the knife struck a rib, and being thin, the blade bent at the handle. When the buffalo regained his feet and loosened himself from the dogs, he turned his attention toward me. I was forced to jump and climb into a thorn beam bush nearby. The buffalo's feet were resting upon the lower limbs some four feet from the ground, and in his anger he made several thrusts with his horns to hook me. The animal struck the trunk of the tree and came near to throwing me off. Fortunately, my dogs continued to worry the buffalo, who finally went off to join its group. I was glad to have escaped and let him go, although the dogs chased him for some time.

A little later there was a severe rain- and windstorm, with lightning and thunder; the storm took down a great deal of timber. I was then near a cliff on the east fork, so I got under the overhanging rocks, safe from the storm and the falling timber. It is generally said by old hunters that bears do not leave their holes in the spring till after they hear heavy thunder and when weeds have gotten started several inches for them to feed upon. Soon after this heavy storm, the very same day, I met and shot a fine bear. Then I saw several others, but before the storm I had seen no bear signs anywhere. At that time I decided to load up my bear meat and go home. Thus I postponed my beaver hunt.

We were not there long before Jonathan Bryan's father came out from the old Kentucky settlements to join his son. The old man and a young stepson, named William Kenshaw, started with me on another beaver hunt to Blaine Creek. One rainy evening, well up the east fork of the Little Sandy and at camp, James Bryan started out alone to hunt. He saw some buffalo and pursued them. Finally he got lost, and the weather continued to be rainy and cloudy for several days. We waited three or four days for him; then young Kenshaw and I returned home with the horses and traps to organize a search party. While so doing, the old man returned. He had followed a creek emptying into the main fork of the Sandy River, following it until he reached the saltworks.

In October of 1796, General Lee of Mason County gave my father a deputy surveyor's commission. This was just before we started on the bear hunt up Sandy River. He had a large tract to survey near the mouth of Blaine Creek. We took one or two persons as chain carriers and started out together. Our party included a couple of young gentlemen named Barlow and Duval from Paris, Kentucky, who had been brought up at their ease. They went along for a woods pleasure excursion. From Limestone we went in a canoe up the Ohio and the Big Sandy Rivers. The surveying lasted several days, and we were miles back from the river. The game was scarce, and while in the woods we ran short of provisions; for the last day or two we had nothing. When the survey was completed, we returned to the canoe, where Father had left his provisions. Among the other articles were some apples and a bottle of "old Monongahela" which we obtained from a boat while traveling from Limestone. Young Barlow and Duval ate plentifully of the green apples with a generous amount of old Monongahela and got quite sick.

In the early part of the fall of 1798, my father, Daniel Boone, moved from the Brushy Fork of Hinkston to my place, located just above the mouth of Little Sandy River. We built a cabin in the woods and at once started clearing the land; we had four or five acres ready for spring crops. Jesse Boone and Philip Goe remained on the Brushy Fork farm. Goe purchased this farm from my father, and there Goe permanently settled. It was there that he and his wife lived and died. Major Andrew Hood and family moved from high up on the Big Sandy River and settled at the mouth of the Little Sandy. Major Hood, his son and a son-in-law, two or three other families, and ourselves made up the settlement in and around there.

In the spring of 1799, my brother Jesse temporarily moved in with my uncle. By then we were preparing to remove to Missouri. Jesse had an unimproved tract just above mine, and as I went off leaving my place unsold, I ask Jesse to sell it or else keep it himself and sell his own land, which he eventually did. Jesse remained there until he finally moved to

Missouri in 1818. For several years before he moved he was the inspector at the saltworks on the Little Sandy River. He was also the aide to General Desha on the 1813 campaign. While living in Greenup County, Jesse [Boone] was a judge and bore the title, probably, of county court.[6]

9

TO MISSOURI

Nathan Boone: About the time my father moved from Point Pleasant to Kentucky, my brother Daniel went down the Mississippi, exploring and examining the country, and hunted and trapped on the upper waters of Tombigbee River. He did not like that country, and his attention was directed towards Missouri. He had heard something about Missouri when going down the Mississippi. In the fall of 1797, he decided to go and see the country. Colonel James Smith, the old pioneer and captive, and Joseph Scholl, my brother Daniel's brother-in-law, agreed to accompany him. Father took an interest in this exploration and even then considered Missouri as his future home. He gave instructions to call on the Spanish governors and make inquiry in his behalf. He wanted to know the quantity of land granted to new settlers, heads of families and children, and servants. He also wanted to know if settlers were required to embrace the Catholic religion. Daniel M. Boone, Colonel Smith, and Scholl traveled by boat down the Ohio to old Fort Massac, then across the country to Kaskaskia and Fort Chartres. In Illinois, Smith and Scholl were not pleased with that country; not caring to go farther, they returned home.

Brother Daniel Boone went on. He examined the Femme Osage in St. Charles District, then called on [Lieutenant] Governor [Zenon] Trudeau, who seemed pleased with the idea of having my father settle in the country as the head of a new colony of emigrants. The governor wrote him a letter on January 24, 1798, expressing his pleasure at the prospect of his settling in Upper Louisiana. He said that if he came, he should have 1,000 arpents of land for himself and that each family who came with him should be entitled to 600 arpents or perhaps 400 for the man, 40 arpents extra for his wife, and 40 acres extra for each child and servant.[1] An unmarried young man would have 400 arpents. Though it was usually required in the Spanish dominions that their citizens should be members of the National Church, it was not enforced so far as American emigrants to Upper Louisiana were concerned. The priests only resided in the towns and dense Spanish settlements, and American settlers were left to enjoy their own religious views but without attempting their propagation.

In the spring of 1799 my brother Daniel appeared at my father's house on the Little Sandy River. He returned from Missouri in 1798 and went back in the fall of the same year, accompanied by his nephew, Philip Goe Jr. They took three Negroes and began the settlement of his grant. He built a good house and left his Negroes to spend the winter in clearing land and preparing for the spring crop. Then he returned to Kentucky to visit Father. This visit, together with the previous letter of Governor Trudeau, convinced my father and me to accompany him back to Missouri. We then started making preparations, as we had just put in our little crop. We found an unusually large poplar tree half a mile up the Little Sandy just below the falls and used it to make a large pirogue. This boat was five feet in diameter and between fifty and sixty feet long. It would hold five tons of our goods and family merchandise. We spent much time in completing the boat, and it was not until fall that we were ready to start.

You may be interested in a story about Tom Hood, the son of Major Andrew Hood. In 1799 while working on the family pirogue in Kentucky, some dogs chased a bear into the Little Sandy near where Tom was standing. Tom, by way of his bravado, instantly leaped upon the bear in the water. The bear didn't like this and, with his paw, pushed Tom under the water every time he came up until he almost drowned him.

Jesse Griffith was on the bank of the stream but was unable to render any aid. The bear finally left the water and went up a tree, where Tom and Griffith killed it. At another time while his dogs were hotly engaged finding a buffalo, Tom climbed up a small linden tree, and as the buffalo passed he jumped down astraddle the animal. Apparently half-frightened and out of its wits, the animal bounded off at the top of its speed. Tom finally had to draw his knife and cut the enraged animal's hamstrings to put a stop to this frightful ride. Tom was simple and daring and sought this kind of notoriety.

In early spring of 1799 I went hunting fifteen or twenty miles up Tygert's Creek, below Greenup, Kentucky, with two Irishmen, George and Robert Buchanan.[2] The dogs flushed a buffalo and the men shot it several times, but when enraged, the buffalo seems more tenacious of life and is hard to kill. Robert Buchanan proposed to knock the buffalo in the head while the dogs held it at bay. This was tried, but his first blow seemed to land in the thick shaggy bunch of hair hanging down in front. He tried again and the buffalo turned on him. Buchanan leaped behind a tree just large enough to shield him as the buffalo charged it several times. Robert urged me to shoot it, but I was laughing so hard I could not aim the gun. George, who was rather green in the woods, was having all he could do to take care of himself. I finally recovered enough to call off the dogs, and the buffalo dropped from weakness and his wounds.

Here I think I should explain why my father left Kentucky. Some of his land locations in the area were made early, and the titles were generally good. But these he mostly sold at low prices, and with the proceeds he purchased additional land warrants and made new entries. Some lands which he sold for a trifle and others which he had even given away were subsequently lost by overlapping claims. In these cases he was compelled to pay damages, often for many times more than the price he sold this land for, when he sold it at all. He gave away a considerable amount of land. I know he gave or exchanged a tract with William Hays and gave another to Joseph Scholl, his sons-in-law, near Boone's Station. At an early date he sold a splendid tract of 1,000 acres, lying between the head of Elkhorn and Boone's Station, to Gilbert Imlay and took his bond for £1,000. Imlay sold this tract to others, then went to England and died there, and Father lost the land, as he was never paid. At Limestone my father gave security for Captain Ebenezer S. Platt for £500 which he had to pay off. He never recovered but a moiety of it. Yet he was so confiding that he loaned this man a Negro, a horse, a saddle, and a bridle, supposedly to go to Louisville on business, but he never heard of him but once afterwards. Captain Platt was in New Orleans, so my father never got his property or its worth again, and this was the only Negro boy my father then possessed.

When he left Kentucky he had for years been troubled with making these lost claims good, or rather paying off amounts greater than those for which he sold them. He had, besides, been frequently called upon to attend courts as a witness to establish some corner tree or survey.[3] Though his testimony was often important, the injured participants would sometimes ungenerously throw out intimations that my father, Daniel Boone, had been bribed or had deviated from the truth. As sensitive as he was, these things greatly annoyed him. About the time he settled at Limestone and shortly before the beginning of the land litigation of Kentucky, he thought himself worth a fortune in the undeveloped lands of Kentucky. He owned considerable property and was thriving and prosperous. Little by little his wealth melted away before these constant claims for damages, and when he finally left Kentucky in 1799 he was poor. But even then, Father still had claims to well-nigh 100,000 acres, but most of it was also claimed by others.[4] He resolved he would never contest their right. He decided to go and leave it all and advised his children who might survive him never to contest these claims. He said that the suits, even if successful, would cost more time, money, and vexation than they would be worth. He never after looked after or inquired about these abandoned claims.

He had one large claim, a half-interest in a 10,000-acre tract. It was located on Licking River, on the northern or eastern bank, at the old Indian trail that crossed the river some eight miles below the Lower Blue Licks. It was in a broken and rather poor country; he had located it in 1782, hence it was not shingled over by other entries. This tract he conveyed to his nephew, Colonel John Grant, to sell or deed by piecemeal to those who might present honest claims against him. To adjust these claims he felt a strong anxiety. How Colonel Grant disposed of the land, Father never troubled himself to inquire; but this tract probably liquidated a few claims.

In some instances, my father's court testimony in land cases so upset those who had lost their claims that they would threaten his life. He often said he could not travel with safety. Even in time of peace he felt his own Kentucky was as dangerous to him as in the time of Indian wars. In addition to premeditated personal injury, he felt he was a target for assassination. He said he thought he had been hardly treated. Though he had fought as hard and long for Kentucky as any other person, he would rather be poor than retain an acre of land or a farthing in money so long as claims and debts hung over him.

General Green Clay wrote to my father on May 4, 1806, from Madison County, Kentucky, and mentioned having received by Captain John Sappington my father's letter about the two claims entered in the name of Robert Clark Jacob.[5] One was near the Blue Licks and the other on the waters of Big Bone Lick Creek. He wrote, "You and your old lady, who I hope is well, are both old and in a new country where there will, of course, be many hardships to encounter, and if you believe that you are able to travel back to Kentucky, and will come and shew the lines, or the corners, or one or two corners and lines of Jacob's two claims, or either of them, I will provide for the support of yourself and your lady all your lives afterwards; and a handsome legacy for you to leave to your children. I will either let you have negroes, or stock, or cash whichever will be your choice to accept, and which you may think will be agreeable to you two. I know you were very ill-treated by many persons for whom you did business, and I also know the great difficulties labored under, and the great distress you suffered by doing business for people who gave you no thanks for your trouble—nor even paid you your just due. These people ought to suffer. I have but a small part in these two tracts of land, and I would willingly divide my interest with you to come at my right!"

But my father, Colonel Daniel Boone, would not go. He said that when he left Kentucky, he did it with the intention of never stepping his feet upon Kentucky soil again; and if he was compelled to lose his head on the block or revisit Kentucky, he would not hesitate to choose the former.

Lyman Draper: How good was your father as a surveyor?

Nathan Boone: He had no problem running simple square or oblong surveys, and he could do the necessary calculations.[6] I would suppose that in the woods he would run a line as straight as the next man.

Draper: Please continue about settling in Missouri.

Nathan Boone: In the middle of September 1799, we packed our big pirogue, and my brother Daniel and I started down the river with our mother in the boat. My father drove the livestock by land, assisted by a young man named George Buchanan and Negro Sam. When we reached Limestone, I got my marriage license and returned seventy-five miles to Little Sandy, where Mrs. Peter Van Bibber then lived, and on September 26 I was married to Miss Olive Van Bibber. We started our move to Missouri on October 1 and went all the way by land, by way of Lexington, Louisville, Vincennes, and St. Louis.

In 1799, when I was married, it grieved the old colonel that he had nothing to give me and my wife with which to start our new life. He lamented his losses and misfortunes, but we thought none the less of him. He was rigidly honest and possessed nice perceptions of justice.

Flanders Callaway, Forest Hancock, Isaac Van Bibber, and William Hays Sr. and Jr. all joined Colonel Boone while he was traveling by land. They fell in with him either at Limestone or at points below. Callaway and Van Bibber also brought livestock. William Hays Sr., Callaway, and Van Bibber with their families joined the boat party. Flanders Callaway Jr., the second son of Flanders Callaway, then about sixteen years old, accompanied his father and grandfather and assisted in driving the cattle from Louisville to Vincennes and St. Louis.[7]

In the boat were my mother, my brother Daniel M. Boone, my uncle, Squire Boone, William L. Boone from Shelby County, Kentucky, James Clay, Robert Hall, and Philip Miller. The three latter men, together with Daniel M. Boone, were then unmarried.

Uncle Squire spent the winter and perhaps a year or two in Missouri, got a grant on Quiver [Cuivre] River, and commenced building a stone house.[8] When it was half built, his two sons came out and persuaded him to leave his house and go back to Kentucky. William L. Boone soon returned without trying to get a grant.

My father, Daniel Boone, reached St. Louis the latter part of October, and the boat party arrived about the same time. He drove the livestock above the mouth of the Missouri, crossed there, and took them to brother Daniel M. Boone's place.[9] He had brought horses, cattle, sheep, and hogs.

He called on [Lieutenant] Governor [Don Charles Dehault] Delassus; the old governor, [Zenon] Trudeau, was still there but had been superseded. Nevertheless, he used his influence and had his promises to my father confirmed. Blank concessions were given to him according to a list of the number of persons accompanying him, leaving him to designate the tracts and fill in the names. And they were antedated to correspond with the time Trudeau had written to and promised my father the concessions in case he would settle in the country; and in order that they might hold good, in case of an expected (and perhaps already agreed on) transfer of jurisdiction of the country from Spain to France. Thus he secured these titles and made them come within the jurisdiction of Spain.

Olive and I had preceded them; we reached St. Louis just after they had gone up the river and proceeded across the country to St. Charles, Missouri.[10] I then returned and met Father at St. Charles. When I met Father there, I discovered I had but half a dollar left, having just purchased some flour, not more than twenty-five pounds, for a guinea. My brother's Negroes had raised some ten or fifteen acres of crops, and so we were comfortably provided for that winter. Both Olive and I and my mother and father spent the winter at brother Daniel's house.[11] We did not make a regular hunt that fall and winter and only went out to kill deer and turkeys for our home supplies of meat. That year the others selected their lands, had them surveyed, and moved to them. My brother's house was on the bluff, a mile back or north of the Missouri and about twenty-five miles above St. Charles village.[12]

My grant was for 400 acres, and it was located about four miles northwest from my brother's, on the northern bank of the Femme Osage and some six or seven miles above its mouth. It was also twenty-five miles from St. Charles Village.[13] I had reached St. Louis after my father, Colonel Daniel Boone, and my name was not included in the list, and so I was not then provided for. Therefore, I purchased the home grant of Robert Hall, for which I gave my only horse, saddle, and bridle, and so subsequently got his concession at Loutre Lick.[14]

At sugar-making time in February my father and mother went to my place and built a half-faced camp (cabins with three sides and the front open) where they made three or four hundred pounds of sugar. It took them several weeks. In the meantime, I built a cabin and cleared eight or nine acres of timberland for my first crop. There was no prairie closer to my land than seven or eight miles.

In March of 1800, my brother Daniel married Sarah Lewis, the daughter of John Lewis. Lewis lived in the Bon Homme settlement on the east side of the Missouri River. It was then entirely an American settlement, composed of John Lewis, John Long, Captain James Mackey, Lawrence Long, Francis Howell, and some other heads of families, mostly

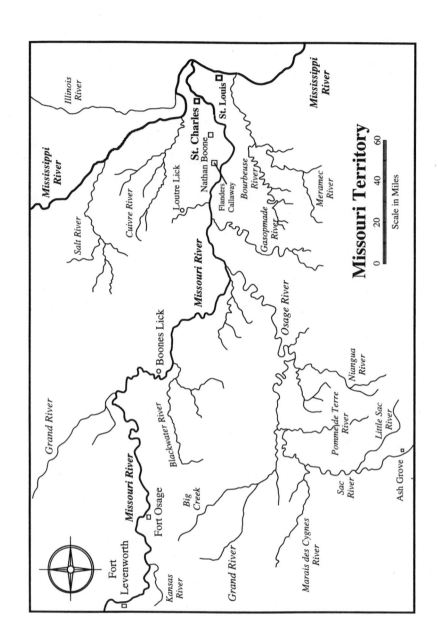

Missouri Territory

0 20 40 60

Scale in Miles

from Kentucky, except Mackey, who was a smart Scotchman.[15] This settlement was started in 1797 or 1798. Sarah died in the summer of 1851, leaving several children. One son died in California and another also moved there.

Joseph Haines, John Lindsay, Joshua Dotson, Samuel Clay, and Samuel Watkins, all young unmarried men, came out to Missouri in the fall of 1798 and settled near my brother. For some time that settlement was known as Bachelor's Bottom. In that period these were the only American settlements in Upper Louisiana.

About 1809, my son, James Boone, was sent to St. Charles to school and boarded at a Frenchman's, but he got homesick. When my father heard of it, he and Mother went down, took a room at St. Charles, and kept house there for some time and made a home for little son James.[16]

In June 1800 my father, Colonel Daniel Boone, was appointed commandant of the Femme Osage District. It was then formed from St. Charles, perhaps on purpose so that the Americans would not be brought before Spanish officers. Christopher Tayon, the commandant of St. Charles, was an unpopular man, as he didn't settle his land grant. He owned all the bottom land lying between my brother Daniel and the Missouri River.

As I recall, the syndic and the commandant were separate offices. The syndic had only civil jurisdiction, whereas the commandant had both civil and military. Capital offenses were tried before the governor. One murderer was sentenced to be set adrift in a canoe in which he was fastened and holes bored in the bottom to die by drowning. We knew this criminal's family.

My father had been exempted by the governor from actually improving his land. By the Spanish law, to obtain a free grant of land the settler must make an actual settlement. He must occupy it himself or with an agent and clear ten acres annually until one-tenth of the whole was improved. The American commissioners rejected my father's claim for want of an actual improvement. I think it was perhaps laid before two sets of commissioners and rejected, or at least not confirmed.

When Father's land claim was not honored by the United States, my brother Jesse suggested he send his petition to Congress. It was perhaps drawn up by Judge [John] Coburn, if he then resided at St. Louis.[17] My father petitioned not for a confirmation of his 1,000-arpent grant, but for a grant of 10,000 acres in consideration of his early services in discovering and settling Kentucky, and he mentioned his losses and poverty. When the petition was sent to Judge Jesse Boone, I sent with it a memorandum of the desired locality of the 10,000 acres on the northern bank of the Missouri, beginning at the mouth of the Big Bonne Femme and chiefly above the Bonne Femme. This was one of the finest tracts of land in Missouri.

The bill to grant Father this land had a good chance of passage, since it was favored by the influential General Joseph Desha from Kentucky. But Mr. [Edward] Hempstead, the Missouri delegate, ignorantly said that some who had spoken in my father's favor were mistaken and that Colonel Boone only asked for a confirmation of his old Spanish grant. He contended that the petition was a misrepresentation as to the amount of land my father had requested. This blunder of Mr. Hempstead's was adopted, as the others thought the Missouri delegate must know fully the merits and facts of the case. So the petition for the 10,000 acres was never discussed. His old claim was confirmed, as it had not been sold; no public lands had yet been put up for sale in Missouri. My father was no doubt vexed—Congress with a show of generosity had not yet given him a grant but merely confirmed his old and rightful claim, which by all rights was already his property. Besides, not long after, Congress passed a law confirming all similar claims. I suspect that the total amount of land my father expected was not stated in his petition, but if not, the amount was in the memo sent with the petition.

From news reports, James Bridges and one or two others learned of Father's proposed grant from Congress and hastened here from Kentucky.[18] They presented their ancient claims against him for lands which he had originally conveyed but titles to which had proved invalid in the courts of Kentucky. For this reason my father, Colonel Daniel Boone, disposed of every acre of his old Spanish grant, which had been confirmed by Congress, to liquidate these demands.

Afterwards no other claimants came out to Missouri from Kentucky except one man, and this was after Father had yielded up the whole tract and had nothing left. My father had once made this man's wife, when an orphan child, a present of a tract of land, and it was subsequently lost to an earlier or more precise entry. Father told the man he should have been satisfied, as the land had not cost him nor his wife anything; at the time he really thought the title was good. It was given in good faith and from charitable feelings when he made the present. Now he owned not a single acre of land on earth and was himself dependent upon his children. Father said even if he wanted to compensate the man, he had nothing to give him. But this fellow would not be satisfied; he still wanted the "pound of flesh" from the old pioneer. My father, Daniel Boone, vexed at the greedy, unfeeling disposition the fellow manifested, finally told him in a quiet way that he thought he had come a great distance to suck a bull, and he reckoned he would have to go home dry. This was the last of the land claimers.[19]

10

HUNTING IN MISSOURI

Nathan Boone: I remember an early hunt conducted by me and Isaac Van Bibber. He afterwards lived at Loutre Lick on the Bourbeuse River or Creek.[1] My father, Daniel Boone, hunted occasionally for amusement around home. He and Mother moved in with my family and in 1805 built a small house in my yard, and there the old couple lived by themselves for several years. They lived there until just before my mother's death in March 1813. In the spring of that year she had, together with my father, gone up to Flanders Callaway's to make maple sugar.

In the summer and early fall of 1801, my brother Daniel and I hunted on the Bourbeuse or Muddy River, killing deer for the skins. That year they brought forty cents per pound in St. Louis by simply taking off the hair and not graining them. Our skins averaged two and a half pounds each.

In the latter part of the summer of 1801 or 1802, my father joined us on a deer hunt for awhile. He then visited a hunting camp of the Shawnee and met Jimmy Rogers and Jackson, whose Indian name was "Fish." They, along with an old squaw, were survivors of his old acquaintances when a prisoner in 1778; and subsequently he visited them at their town near Owen's Station, which was located about twelve miles northwest of St. Louis, near Florissant.[2]

I remember when my father went beaver trapping on the Bourbeuse with Derry, a twenty-two-year-old Negro boy belonging to my brother, who liked to go out with Father while he trapped. Derry would stretch the skins and acted as cook and camp tender. In the fall of 1801 my brother and I went on a more distant hunt upon the Niango River, then called the Youngo by the French and Spanish. It was an easterly branch of the Grand Osage.[3] We found plenty of beaver. That year we returned home with approximately one hundred beaver skins, some deer skins, and some bear. We met no Indians.

In the spring of 1802 William T. Lamme and I returned to the Niango River.[4] We had a very good beaver hunt in the same area where we had hunted the year before. Two hatters from Lexington came to Missouri to buy furs, and our family and Lamme sold them their furs. William T. Lamme was a son-in-law of Flanders Callaway.

In mid-September of 1802, I went with William T. Lamme on a big hunt. We hunted some on the Big Pomme de Terre, then crossed the Osage and made our principal hunt on a northerly branch of Grand River.[5] We caught nine hundred beavers but lost about one hundred when Indians found them cached. But we saw no Indians. I took the furs to Lexington, Kentucky, and sold them for $2.50 each.

In October 1802, my father, Daniel Boone, accompanied by Derry, took his grandson, William Hays Jr., and joined Flanders Callaway and his son James for a fall and winter's hunt along the Niango River. There they separated, with the Callaways making one party; my father, Hays, and Derry another. They trapped on the Big Niango and Pomme de Terre but stayed a few miles apart. One day while Hays was absent trapping and Father had just ridden away from camp to look at traps, a party of eight or ten Osages came running toward the camp yelling and shooting off their guns. Derry took to his heels and hid. My father saw that the Indians were firing into the air, no doubt trying to frighten him and Derry away so they could take the goods from their camp.

My father rode back to camp, and the Indians pulled him from his horse and took his capeau coat.[6] However, they were not openly hostile, so he called Derry back to camp. Derry managed to secrete a chunk of lead and Boone had a supply of powder concealed. The Indians took their furs, Father's capeau coat, the powder in his horn, etc. They also had Derry cook a meal for them. Afterwards Father and Derry had enough hidden ammunition left to kill meat, so they remained trapping until spring. They finally came home with about two hundred beaver skins.

The Callaways also had fair success and took my father's furs along with theirs to sell in Lexington. His share was about a hundred [dollars?], and he used the proceeds to liquidate certain old debts including a balance due merchants in Lexington. But Father never went himself to

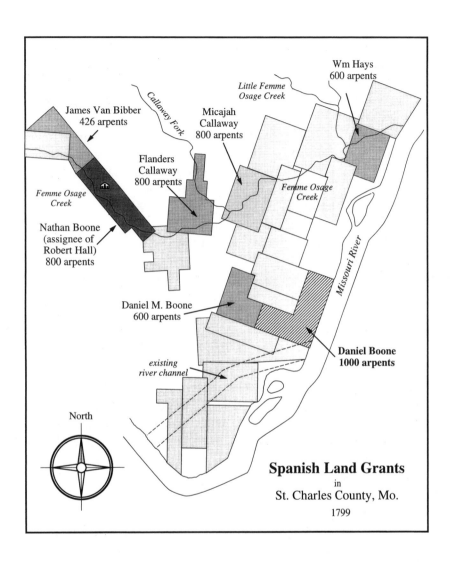

James Van Bibber
426 arpents

Micajah
Callaway
800 arpents

*Little Femme
Osage Creek*

Wm Hays
600 arpents

Flanders
Callaway
800 arpents

Callaway Fork

*Femme Osage
Creek*

*Femme Osage
Creek*

Nathan Boone
(assignee of
Robert Hall)
800 arpents

Daniel M. Boone
600 arpents

Missouri River

**Daniel Boone
1000 arpents**

*existing
river channel*

North

Spanish Land Grants
in
St. Charles County, Mo.
1799

Kentucky as Peck says and as the romance of a land witness story of Audubon relates.

After this trip my father made no distant hunts for some time, but he hunted around home a little. He suffered some from rheumatism for a couple of years.

In the fall of 1803 I went hunting with William T. Lamme, James Fair, and James and John Callaway. We went to the Niango River and had four horses stolen by Indians.[7] We trapped on the Niango and Grand Rivers, then crossed to the Kansas and made station camp some sixty or eighty miles from the mouth, at the mouth of the Wah-ha-roosa, which joined the Kansas on the south and east side. Lamme and I hunted together. It was a good hunt even though Indians carried off a considerable proportion of our furs.

In 1804 Matthias Van Bibber and I started on a winter's hunt, aiming to go to the Kansas [River]. I had caught fifty-six beavers and twelve otters when a party of twenty-two Osage Indians came to our camp one day. They took our three horses and what furs we had and told us we had better clear out, as there was another party hunting for us, and then they departed.

A few minutes later another party came yelling towards the camp, so we ran and hid ourselves in the bush. Finally the Indians went away. Van Bibber and I moved eight or ten miles away and camped again. Early the next morning we killed a deer and were cooking it when four Indians came walking into camp. We ordered them off at gunpoint, but they said they were Sauks so were permitted to come in and eat. After a while these Indians attempted to snatch our guns, but we prevented this thievery, but Van Bibber and I took to the trees.

After some time, a compromise was reached, and we finally started off in company with those Indians. Soon other Indians joined them. Then one struck me with a ramrod, and instantly both we and the Indians cocked rifles, all within a few feet of each other. The situation developed into a standoff. The Indians were more numerous, but they didn't want to lose two of their men to take us. Finally the Indians said if we would give them powder, balls, and flints, they might go.

Van Bibber and I agreed to provide the Indians with these items if they would lay down their guns and come up one at a time to receive their portion. This was done, and the Indians moved off. As soon as the

Indians were out of sight over a ridge, Van Bibber and I struck off at a run and kept running till after dark. We had only five bullets between us but more powder in proportion. We had lost our blankets and coats, which were on the horses the Indians took, but we felt it wiser not to try to recover them. We were now in shirtsleeves. This robbery occurred November 26 or 27. The next morning we shot a turkey.

Soon snow began to fall. We traveled two days and struck the Missouri River. We managed to cross on the ice and continued on down. It snowed for two or three days and became knee-deep. We shot away our remaining four balls but killed nothing, as our guns seemed to be affected by the cold weather. We were seventeen days without meat, eating only grapes and haws, some of which were still found in the woods and thickets. Finally we tried cutting up our wiping sticks and using them as bullets to shoot at game, but we had no success. We finally came to an old Indian camp and found where the Indians had shot at a mark. We cut enough lead out of the tree to make four balls. Two or three miles further we came to some old Indian cabins, which were perhaps half a mile below where Rocheport now stands.[8] It was getting on towards night, so we decided to go into one of the cabins, make a fire, and stay till morning.

When we were twenty or thirty miles before reaching the Indian camps, we came upon what is now Boone's Lick. Here are several springs of saltwater and a spring branch that runs a mile or two and then sinks into the alluvial soil of the Missouri bottom. Some Indian hunters had seen it, and Captain James Mackey had either seen it or got information and laid a preemption on it, but he did not get a grant for failing to make the required improvement. Subsequently James Morrison laid a preemption right on the land, including the springs, and purchased the tract from the government at $1.25 per acre. Captain Mackey was the first American to go and visit the Mandan Indians to see if they were the Welsh Indians. He spent some time with them about 1801 but concluded they were not descended from Welsh stock, though they had fairer skin than many other Indians. On this trip he may have discovered this famous lick.

On entering the Indian cabin, I was in the lead and spied a huge panther lying on his belly, some ten feet distant. I shot and killed it, skinned it, and roasted it on stick spits. This animal had a sweet and cattish taste. I cut the skin into two pieces, and we each made a vest, cutting holes for inserting our arms and wearing the fur side next to our bodies. We fastened our fur vests with strings, and though our arms were still exposed, they added vastly to our comfort. We were now greatly revived, and hoppusing up [tying onto our backs] the balance of our meat, the next morning we started again. We had only traveled three or four miles when we discovered a person's tracks in the snow. We decided to follow them to their camp, regardless of whether they were white or Indian.

In a mile and a half we came to the weather-bound camp of a party of white hunters consisting of my nephew, James Callaway, and three or four other friends and acquaintances. This was a time of inexpressible joy for the two hapless wanderers. We had, from time to time, as our moccasins were worn through by the frozen snow and ice, cut off a sufficiency of the lower part of our deerskin leggings for patch-leather—until finally our leggings were nearly gone and our legs entirely exposed to the severity of the weather. At this camp we obtained good buffalo and deer meat, clothing, blankets, and ammunition from this group. We recruited for a week with them, then resumed our hundred-mile journey home.

The weather moderated, and we had no difficulty on the way home. I reached home on December 24 and spent Christmas with my family and parents.

Olive Boone: It was the first Christmas he had spent at home since our marriage, and I had to thank the Indians for that.

Nathan Boone: I have never fully recovered from the effects of the exposure and suffering, and poor Van Bibber never after enjoyed good health. Two or three years later he died on Gauley River in Western Virginia.

In the spring of 1805 I went alone to the Osages to try to recover my horses, furs, etc., which had been taken from me. I first went to the Big Osage town on Pomme de Terre Creek, about six miles from the Osage River. There I found a trader and discovered it was the Little Osage Indians who had robbed me. Then I went to the Little Osage town, about six miles from the Big Osage town on a fork of the Pomme de Terre. The chief of the whole Osage tribe was White Hair, who lived at Big Osage town. He tried to seize my horses, but I got them out of the way. I remained there seventeen days but recovered only two traps, so I left.

I had hired a young man to go with me to watch the horses and traps, who was left some forty miles from the Indian towns. This young man was supposed to trap while I was gone but was afraid, so he stayed at camp and had not trapped any. When I got back from the Indian towns we packed up my traps and returned home.

In the spring of 1800 I built this cabin. It was small, without a floor, and as the spring rains began, water came in. Occasionally the puddles on the floor were several inches deep. My dear wife, Olive, and her Negro girl got poles to lay down for string pieces, then peeled elm bark and laid it down as a floor, the rough side up to prevent its warping or rolling up. That winter and spring she and her Negro girl cut all the wood and fed the cattle while my father and I were absent hunting. When she wanted a sieve, she peeled a piece of bark from a hickory tree, bent it together to a proper size in circular shape, lapped the ends, and stitched them with bark strings. She then tanned a deer skin with ashes, stretched it tightly over the hoop, and fastened it securely. Then with a heated wire she burned holes through the skin and then had a sieve which answered a very good purpose.

In the summer of 1800, I erected a good substantial log house, and several years after that I replaced it with a commodious stone building.[9] My father, Daniel Boone, built himself a shop and had a set of tools, and when at home he would make and repair traps and guns. In fact he did all the needed smith work for the family and sometimes for neighbors to oblige them. But after a few years he disposed of his tools. My wife, Olive, had a loom but no convenient place to put it, so she took possession of the deserted shop while my father and I were away hunting. The weather was cold, and there was no fireplace in the old shop; the Negro girl was sent to the nearest neighbor a mile off to obtain the loan of a crosscut saw, with which Olive and the girl cut through several courses of logs until a suitable-sized aperture for a fireplace was made. Then with stones for the fireplace, sticks for the chimney, and mud for mortar these lone women erected a chimney, the draft of which proved decidedly the best of any on the farm. Upon our return home we could scarcely believe the story of these architects.

In spite of reports to the contrary, my father never discovered Boone's Lick.[10] It took its name from the fact that my brother and I worked there and from brother Dan's early discovery of it. In 1806 we began making salt there. We employed six or eight men and had one furnace with forty kettles. This saltworks produced twenty-five or thirty bushels of salt per day. The salt was boated down to the settlements and at St. Louis usually sold for $2.00 to $2.50 per bushel.

Afterward we enlarged the furnace and also erected a new one, having sixty kettles in each to increase the size, and kept from sixteen to twenty men employed making one hundred bushels of salt per day. These springs had never been worked by white or red men before. It took about three hundred gallons of the water to make a bushel of salt. We made what was a nice experiment, performed with care and saving, and when not allowed to boil over and waste, proved that 250 gallons of water could make a bushel. Before the working at Boone's Lick, Charles Gratiot, at Gratiot's Licks on the Merrimack, located a few miles up from St. Louis, had made salt on a small scale with weak water. These two works were the only ones in operation for many years in Missouri.

Lyman Draper: According to the notes of George Rogers Clark, there was an earlier saltworks near St. Genevieve in 1778.

Nathan Boone: Perhaps so, but I have never heard of it. In any event, we manufactured salt at Boone's Lick for nearly four years, but it did not prove to be profitable. I quit first, and my brother Daniel then sold out his interest to James Morrison.

In 1805 the Osage Indians killed some frontier people, and their principal chief, White Hair, came to General William Clark and said he could not control them. Clark said let the peaceable ones come live on the Missouri River, and a fort (Fort Osage) would be provided for their protection. Let the others go to war if they wished. I was selected to guide General Clark and a body of troops to the Fire Prairie where they built Fort Osage. The Indians didn't come in as expected, and Clark sent me to the Osage towns. I was treated rudely there, but he insisted on waiting for their answer, and finally several hundred, at White Hair's urging, went and made a treaty.[11]

In the fall of 1811, I went out spying with Lewis Jones and early in March 1812 was appointed captain of Rangers. That is when I disposed of my interest in the saltworks. The saltworks could have been a profitable business except for the trouble and pilfering of the Indians. For several years, they kept stealing and killing the beef cattle. We need these cattle to feed the workers, and when they were taken by Indians the works would have to stop until we could send some 150 miles to the settlements and buy and bring up others. This was tedious matter; and the hands in the meantime would do nothing. But the salt bore a good price.

About the fall of 1808, my father, Daniel Boone, took his grandson, William Hays Jr., and Derry on a fall and winter beaver hunt. They departed with four or five horses to ride out and pack back in. They reached the south side of the Missouri and crossed the Osage and the Lemine Rivers, intending to go on the Kansas River.[12] Near where Independence now stands they met a lone Indian.

By signs this Indian invited my father and his party to his camp. They decided to accept his offer. They followed the Indian to very near his camp when he, with signs, informed them he would like to ride the lead packhorse. My father allowed him to do so; but when within sight of the camp, the Indian dashed ahead, alerted the camp, and twenty or thirty Indians came whooping out. My father and his party wheeled their horses and escaped but had to cut loose their traps and the few skins and furs they had taken.

My father later became ill and, fearing he might not recover, gave instructions to Hays and Derry to bury him between two certain trees near camp. They had intended to go to the Kansas River, where I had previously been. This Indian robbery took place some ten or twelve miles south of the Missouri River, on the head of Sniabar [Little Schuyte Aber] Creek, about twelve or fifteen miles southwest of what is now Lexington, Missouri.[13]

The only dog my father had with him followed the horse which the Indian stole. He had this horse, Old Grey, for a number of years, and it was quite old. The party returned without any furs; the trip was a complete failure.

The following spring my father came to Boone's Lick and got me to accompany him and go search for his lost traps. I went with him, but we failed to find the traps and immediately returned.

In June 1851 the Negro Derry died of flux in Marthasville, Montgomery County, Missouri. He was seventy-two years old. He was a good Negro. He would relate with much gusto stories about his two hunting trips with Father, especially the difficulties they had with the Indians, always giving himself the precedent in the narrative.

William Hays Jr. died at his residence near Fulton, Callaway County, Missouri, a few years since.[14] He was born in Boone's Station in Kentucky in 1780.

During my father's home hunts, while he was yet robust, he would hoppus home his deer; that is, he would fasten it upon his back and thus convey it home.

The statement in Allen's *American Biographical Dictionary* that my father visited the headwaters of the Arkansas River is a mistake. Likewise the story that he erected a cabin on the waters of the Grand Osage in 1810 is also a mistake. The latter statement must refer to my settlement on the Femme Osage in 1799, when Father was living with me. His beaver hunt, mentioned in Irving's *Astoria* (vol. 1, p. 154), must have been the trip he made in 1802.[15]

11

THE WAR OF 1812

Nathan Boone: Towards the close of 1811, the Indians killed the Neal family, his wife and several children, who were living on the Mississippi River near Salt River. Prior to this, Lewis Jones and I were sent out to spy and went up towards the head of Loutre Creek. Soon after the attack on Neal's family, we went into that region and scouted above Neal's residence. Then, in the latter part of the winter of 1811-1812, Governor William Clark wrote and ordered me to raise a company of rangers for three months' service, which I did. My commission bears the date March 27, 1812, and is signed by President Madison.

In 1812 I went to join Colonels Russell and Edwards on their expedition above Peoria.[1] On the way I met some boats below Peoria whose occupants told me the Indian village had been attacked and the Indians had fled, so I returned home.[2]

Shortly after I raised a company and we marched up the Mississippi accompanied by General Benjamin Howard and established Fort Mason, located about fifteen miles above the mouth of Salt River on the west bank of the Mississippi.[3] When the fort was completed, we ranged chiefly between the Mississippi and the Missouri Rivers. At the expiration of the three months, I returned home and raised another company. This was June, and the service was for twelve months. We went out again under the command of General Howard. Our duty was still ranging, scouting, and protecting the frontiers. The term of the men's enlistment expired in June 1813, and we were then discharged; but I was not notified to cease duty, and General Howard gave me the command of three companies, with the rank of a major, though I received only captain's pay.

In August 1813, I took seventeen men to scout a route for the army to march against the Indian towns near Peoria, Illinois. We started from below Cape au Grais, below Fort Mason, and on the second day we camped between the Mississippi and Illinois Rivers. We saw no Indian signs. That night the sentinel detected Indians about, and they seemed to be trying to surround the camp, which was in the woods on a small branch. I doubled the sentinels and ordered all the men away from the fire and to trees around the camp, since they didn't know what direction the attack would come from. Then a man named White and an Indian, who were close to each other, fired simultaneously. White was wounded in both hands and lost both thumbs.

The attack became general, and another man was slightly wounded in the shoulder. Captain James Callaway, son of Flanders Callaway, was in the affair. During this skirmish we lost about half our horses and returned to the fort at Cape au Grais.

In September 1813, General Howard went beyond Peoria [Illinois] and burned several Indian towns that the Indians had abandoned. There he found and took their buried corn. After he returned to Peoria, I was detached with about one hundred men to go to Rock River, but we returned without discovering any Indians.[4] Major William Christy, late of St. Louis and formerly of the Pittsburg region, who was about twelve years older than I, was detached up the Illinois River by water to the mouth of Fox River, now Ottawa, but he made no discoveries.

Colonel Robert Nicholas of Bellefontaine took about 100 men up to Peoria a few days ahead of General Howard, and he was attacked by about 150 Indians. His men pushed their boats into the lake, anchored them, and fired swivel guns at the Indians. This dispersed them. Some of these Indians were the same as those who had attacked our group. They were wearing some of my men's hats. I think these two affairs happened in 1814, certainly not earlier than 1813. I served as major in both campaigns.

In 1814 the upper post at Prairie du Chien surrendered to the British colonel McKay after some days besieging.[5] Before the surrender, Captain James Callaway, Captain Riggs, and Lieutenant Campbell of the infantry went up in three boats with 100 to 150 men; they were attacked in the upper rapids at Rock River and Island just above the mouth of Rock River by British and Indians and driven back. They lost one boat burned, but the men were taken off. About eighteen were killed in this affair, and Lieutenant Campbell was badly wounded. Just before the attack a man named Pitman rolled himself up in his blanket and lay down on the top of one of the boats and never was seen afterwards. He was supposed to have been shot and rolled into the water. This was known as Campbell's defeat.

Immediately thereafter Captain Zachary Taylor went up to the lower end of the same rapids and was also driven back with little or no loss; and he learned from paroled men who had returned that Prairie du Chien had been surrendered to the British.[6] The enemy had a small cannon, and Taylor's boats attempted to land to attack them but could not do so safely, as his boats were exposed to the fire of these British cannon. The enemy was stronger than he expected.

Mrs. Ramsey was killed perhaps in the spring of 1814. She lived about a mile from Charette. The Indians rushed the house and shot her and Mr. Ramsey in the yard, but he recovered. There were two or three children there besides the Ramsey family. He managed to get into the house and held them off.

The sinkhole affair occurred a day or two afterwards. There was a small neighborhood fort located two or three miles above Cuaver River, under the river bluff. The Indians waylaid the place at a pond where the whites got their water, and killed two men. Then Captain [John] Craig, who commanded the fort, took thirty men and pursued the Indians about half a mile to where they had formed an ambuscade. There they attacked Craig's party as they came up. It was in the woods, and the whites took shelter behind trees and fought for some time. At the same time Captain David Musick, whose force was camped near the banks of the Cuaver River grazing their horses, about a mile or a mile and a quarter from the ambuscade, heard the firing and ordered his men to mount. They rushed to the fight and joined in the action.

Soon after Musick's arrival, the Indians broke up. One half of them retreated, while the other half took a post in a large sinkhole about fifty or sixty feet in diameter and some ten or twelve feet deep. Where a lower strata of rocks appeared, there was a cave. Captain Craig was killed about the time that Musick's men arrived, so Musick took command. The Indians had moved between Craig's company and the fort, so when Musick came up, he and his company had to dash through the enemy, at which time Musick and several of his men were wounded.

Captain Musick ordered his men to surround the sinkhole; however, to his surprise, he discovered the Indians were quite secure there and could fire on him with little or no exposure. He tried cannon fire but with no effect. Then a moving battery was prepared, placed on the forewheels of a wagon, and pushed up to fire through portholes in the battery. When the Indians fired at the portholes, Lieutenant Spears and one or two others were killed and some wounded. Some were shot in the legs, which were exposed by the opening beneath the battery. The Indians took refuge in the cave where they had a drum and fife. They kept playing and shooting. This continued till about dusk. The Indians who had retreated to their canoes below the hills along the Mississippi made a feint at the fort. Captain Musick then marched his men off to relieve the fort, and all the Indians departed. About seven or eight Indians were found dead on the battleground and in the sinkhole, but about twelve white soldiers were killed or wounded. This was called the Battle of the Sinkhole.

In the spring of 1815, a party of Indians stole horses from Cole's settlement, located a few miles above Loutre Island on the north side of the Missouri. A neighborhood party, including several Coles, pursued them. The Indians, also mounted, were discovered but kept just ahead and out of shooting range. The pursuers finally turned back and camped for the night on a small branch at the head of Loutre Creek in a little timber. Some decided to sleep away from the fire for safety, including Stephen Cole, who lay behind a log. The Indians returned and attacked during the night. Stephen Cole saw his brother, Temple Cole, in a scuffle with an Indian, so he came to his aid with his knife. For this effort Stephen received several knife wounds from various Indians. He finally was forced to leave his brother, who by then was disabled by a bad wound. Stephen Cole's wounds were serious, but he finally recovered. They had five white men slain, including two named Patton. Only Stephen Cole and James Moredock escaped. Moredock, who had bragged about his prowess in case of Indian attack, had run off at the onset and hidden under the bank of the branch until the Indians departed.

Shortly after the Cole affair, about May 1, 1815, the Indians came into the Loutre Island settlement and stole fifteen or twenty horses. Captain James Callaway and his company were stationed on the island and pursued them about forty miles with about twenty men. Eventually they came to the Indian encampment, where they found the horses but no Indians. They took the horses and, upon examination, discovered the Indians had again headed towards the settlement. Captain Callaway made a forced march with the horses and ran into the Indians, who were returning after attacking the settlement a second time. In this attack they had killed a man and wounded another. The Indians had seen the oncoming whites and ambushed them on the trail. Captain Callaway and one of his men had stopped momentarily behind the others, and when they heard the firing, the other man suggested they make their escape. Callaway refused and rode up to assist the others. He received three wounds, the worst through the groin. His men were defeated with six killed, but the rest escaped. Callaway's horse was killed under him. One of his men tried to take him on behind, but the horse wouldn't permit it. The man had to ride on to save himself; Callaway ran to the nearby creek, the Prairie Fork of Loutre, jumped into a deep hole in the creek, and was shot in the head by the Indians.

The third day after Callaway's defeat, I was with the party who visited the battleground. We buried the dead, all of whom had been scalped and mutilated. A few days later, Flanders Callaway, the father of Captain James Callaway, visited the spot, found his son's unmutilated body in the water, and buried him on the bank of the stream. James Callaway left a wife and three children; he was born about 1783. He had been a member of the Missouri Territorial Council, sheriff, and collector of St. Charles County. He was a popular and useful citizen. From the signs, the Indians who attacked Callaway's party consisted of about forty Sauks and Foxes.

At the Femme Osage settlement, there was a neighborhood fort at Daniel M. Boone's, four miles from my house. The fort and picketing enclosed my brother's house. In time of alarm the neighbors would retreat to this fort. Twice my father, mother, and my family fled there in the dead of night. There were Indian alarms from 1811 until into 1815.

The Indians would often have a dried deer skin with small holes plentifully inserted along the edge by which to fasten it on a hoop to use as a canoe. In these little boats they would put a gun and budget and swim behind, pushing it over the stream. When dry, they would use it as a blanket at night. This was quite customary.[7]

12

THE LAST YEARS

Nathan Boone: Early in 1813 my father and mother went up to Flanders Callaway's at the mouth of Charette Creek, located within a mile of Marthasville, on the Missouri.[1] Their place was twelve miles from my house. In 1799 Flanders Callaway had settled within a mile of me and remained there seven or eight years. My parents went up to Callaway's to aid in sugar making, as he had a good sugar camp. Mother, while there, camped at the sugar camp, which was four miles from Callaway's residence, up Charette Creek, and she remained there about a month. When she was not feeling well, she rode to Callaway's house, and after a few weeks of sickness, she died there, on March 18, 1813.

Afterward, my father returned to the Femme Osage settlement, and he and Callaway decided to pack up their goods and take shelter at my brother Daniel's fort. They went by land, and the goods were sent by water. In one of the canoes there were two or three whites and two Negroes, and they unfortunately ran against an obstruction and upset, thus losing much of the load. Among the articles was my father's manuscript narrative, dictated by him and written down by his grandson John B. Callaway, who was then living on his father's (Flanders Callaway's) place.

At one period, a hired man, Alexander Logan, came here and said he had seen an Indian a quarter of a mile off. My wife was alarmed, but Father was cool and collected and disbelieved the report. He questioned Logan about what the Indian had been doing. Logan said picking off ticks from himself. My father then told Logan he now knew he was a liar, for whenever he saw an Indian that distance in the settlements, he would not catch him picking off ticks.

By April 1816, my father, Daniel Boone, was anxious to make another hunt. He hired a man to accompany him. This fellow was a noted woodsman known by the name of Indian Philips, who frequently would go and live a while with the Indians. He was lazy and indolent and possessed much of the Indian character. The two started up the Missouri in a canoe, reached the mouth of the Grand River, and proceeded up the Grand or Iowa River about eight or ten miles, as far as Coal Banks. They hoped to find beaver there, but the Indian and French trappers had pretty much cleaned them out. They went back to the Missouri again and traveled up some twenty miles above Fort Leavenworth, which had just been established. Then my father became sick, and so he returned to Ft. Leavenworth and there remained a few days. While at the fort he became acquainted with Captain Bennett Riley of the army, who was then in command. He recovered sufficiently to return home, and Phillips returned with him. What Peck says in his book on page 175 cannot be true. My father never made a beaver hunt up the Missouri alone, so I cannot think the details are true.

After my father lost his first narrative manuscript in the river, he stayed awhile with Dr. John Jones's family, near Marthasville, whose wife was a daughter of Flanders Callaway and my father's granddaughter. He went there for the double purpose of placing himself under the doctor's medical care and advice for the scrofulous affection that sometimes bothered him and also to dictate to the doctor a narrative of his life and adventures. Dr. Jones intended to prepare it for press, with the profits to go to my father, Daniel Boone. His life was taken in rough notes, down to the period when he migrated to Missouri. Because of my father's Loutre Lick trip and subsequent sickness and changes of residence among his children, the narrative was never completed. After my father's death, the doctor said repeatedly that no one on earth should have the narrative but me. He said I was entitled to it, but in 1839 he showed it to Ben Howard Boone, my son, who was to hand it over to me. This, however was never done. Dr. Jones suddenly died about 1842, and the narrative disappeared. Benjamin made inquiries about it to Dr. Jones's heirs and executors but without getting any clue about it.

In the fall of 1817, late in November, my father, Daniel Boone, then entered upon his eighty-fourth year, started on a hunting trip with his grandson James Boone, my oldest son. This was before Jesse Boone moved to the country. They started with each mounted on horseback. Upon leaving Flanders Callaway's they proceeded on and camped the first night on the headwaters of Charette, about thirteen miles from Callaway's house. Night overtook them sooner than they expected, and they camped rather late and had not time to prepare a shelter. That night two inches of snow fell. The snow and glare of the fire caused a wild duck to land beside the fire, and James Boone caught it easily, to his bewilderment. Father was exhilarated to be camping out again. He had brought his gun, his kettle, a light axe, provisions, and two or three traps. He seemed to feel himself in his ancient element. After the evening meal he told stories of his "olden time" adventures.

The pair had the duck for breakfast the next morning and continued on their way. The weather had become cold and blustery, so they had to stop and make a fire for Father to warm himself. They went only eight miles that day and stopped at a house of entertainment at Camp Branch, a noted camping place for travelers. The next day they went twenty-two miles to Loutre Lick. The weather had moderated a little but was still cold, and all but two miles of that day's travel was on the exposed prairie. The cold had affected my father's aged frame, and he found he could proceed no further since he could not bear the exposure. He then decided to remain at his granddaughter's, Mrs. Major Van Bibber's, at Loutre Lick and abandon the intended hunt.

It was his original intention to have gone to the headwaters of Loutre Creek, some twenty miles above the lick, and then go across some ten miles to the nearest or south fork of Salt River. Here they expected to find bear, deer, and turkeys, and perhaps some chance buffalo and beaver, and to stay a few weeks, snugly encamped. My father said he was as naturally inclined each fall to go hunting and trapping as the farmer is in spring to set about putting in his crops.

In a day or two James Boone returned home; the old colonel, from his weakness and the inclemency of the weather, didn't think it prudent to attempt returning at that time. A few days later he was alarmingly ill and was thought to be dying. I was told of the situation, and not supposing by the word brought by the messenger that my father could be living, I gave directions before leaving home for a coffin to be made so the funeral might take place immediately on my return. But upon reaching Loutre Lick in a light carriage, I was agreeably surprised to find my father not only living but recovering from his attack. In a few days he was able to ride home.

When we returned, he went to see the coffin that had been hastily provided for him. He thought it too rough and uncouth, and soon after he had a much better one made of cherry, according to his own directions. He took it to my house and kept it in the attic, greatly to the fear of all the little folks in the house. He would frequently visit and inspect it to see that no injury or accident befell it. Morgan Boone, a relative but a stranger, visited us and died in the Charette settlement and was buried in the first coffin. The other received the mortal remains of my father, Colonel Daniel Boone.

In his old age when his hearing became hard, when he saw strangers approaching my house, he, anticipating their prying curiosity, would take his cane and walk off to avoid them. But he retained his mild disposition to the last.

My father was sick off and on after the Loutre Lick trip. During the whole summer of 1820, he was at the Callaway's. There his portrait was painted by Mr. Harding. Everyone thought it good, except that it didn't show his plump cheeks, a sign of the broad face he had in his robust days.

He had an attack of fever, not severe, and while recovering was exceedingly anxious to be taken to my house. My wife and I visited the old man, and he insisted on going back with us. He directed me to get a couple of long poles and fasten them to a couple of horses with a bed swung across, as wounded men were carried on campaigns in the Indian country. This sling was swung over the horses' backs, one horse several feet before the other, with a blanket placed across the poles. I obeyed his instructions and got the litter ready, when Dr. Jones came in and said he must not be transported. The doctor decided he was too feeble and might die on the way. The trip was then postponed two or three weeks.

Finally I took him back in a carriage, and my two little sons, Howard and John, six and four years of age, came along. We reached my house at midday, and he was cheerful and in good spirits. He told his grandchildren he thought he would soon be well enough to go with them and gather some of the hazelnuts he had seen nearby along the road. During the afternoon he enjoyed the innocent prattle of his grandchildren, and to please them he would eat some cakes, nuts, and even drink buttermilk they affectionately presented to him. In this way, it was afterward thought, he loaded his stomach with articles too rich and gross.

But my father rested pretty well that night. The next morning he went out upon the porch, looked around at the farm, and said if he felt as well the next day as he then did, he would ride horseback around the farm. He was brought in and lay down on the bed and slept. Before he awakened, it was discovered that a fever was coming upon him, and he began to complain of an acute burning sensation, such as he never before felt, in his breast, which continually grew worse. When he was advised to take medicine, he declined, as he thought it would do no good. He said it was his last sickness, but, he said calmly, he was not afraid to die. He recognized all his relatives who came to see him during his last sickness and talked until within a few minutes of his last breath. Some ten minutes before he breathed his last, his daughter Mrs. Callaway arrived. He recognized her and died placidly, only exhibiting a scowl with his last breath. Towards the last when asked if he suffered pain, he would say he did in his breast and between his shoulders. He died on the morning of September 26, 1820, about sunrise—the fourteenth day after his arrival here.

Father's body was conveyed to Flanders Callaway's home at Charette, and there the funeral took place. There were no military or Masonic honors, the latter of which he was a member, as there were then but very few in that region of the country. The Reverend James Craig of the Baptist denomination, my son-in-law, delivered the funeral discourse. There was a very large funeral, and the remains were buried beside those of his wife, a mile below Charette Creek and on the elevated second bank of the Missouri, a mile from the river.

In his latter years my father was a great student of the Bible. He was seldom seen reading any other book and fully believed in the great truths of Christianity. He seemed most partial towards the Presbyterians, although he disliked the unkind differences too frequently manifested by different Christian sects. He had all his children, when he could, regularly christened. His worship was in secret, and he placed his hopes in the Savior. Whenever preaching was in his neighborhood, he made it a point to attend and well remembered what he heard and read.

In middle life, he read considerably in history, which was his favorite reading. He did not care for novels.

The Missouri grave marker of Daniel and Rebecca Boone.

My father, Daniel Boone, was five feet, eight inches high and had broad shoulders and chest and tapered down. His usual weight was about 175 pounds, but at one period he exceeded 200 and in his closing years weighed only about 155 pounds. His hair was moderately black, eyes blue, and he had fair skin. He never used tobacco in any form and was temperate in everything. My mother never used tobacco nor raised tobacco, and for this reason I would discredit the tobacco story as related by Peck.[2]

APPENDIX A

Nathan Boone's Letter

Memo: The following was written by Colonel Nathan Boone in response to my several inquiries—& handed to me by him when I visited him, Sept. & Oct. 1851. Lyman C. Draper

1. Daniel Boone was born Berks County, Pa., Oct. 22, 1734. His ancestors Quakers. Daniel himself was brought up with those religious views untill about 17 or 18 years old. He was son of Squire Boone who with two other brothers came from England under govenor Pen about the year 1699 and married in America.

2. Daniel's father kept a dairy some distance from the farm. He went there in summer and fall. Daniel was made the herdsman from the time he was 10 yrs old untill the January left Pensylvania at a boish 17 years of age. Says Daniel's father bought him a gun when he was about 12 or 13, that he soon became expert in killing game and often neglected his duty to bring up the latter. This thing of being a herdsman and rambling through the wood first gave him an idea of the wood & becoming a hunter. He had little or no education but he could Read and Spell a little—which was Taught him by his Sister-in law Samuel Boone's wife. He was between 17 & 18 when family moved to North Carolina.

3. I don't know certainly that Daniel Boone ever resided in Virginia before going to North Carolina.

4. Daniel Boone took no part in the French and Indian wars which extended to the Carolinas. He was out under General G. Washington and General Braddock in 1755 against Fort Duqu[the rest of this word

is missing] not as a soldier but a teamster—[note in margin says: "On this campaign he obtained from a Trader (name not recollected) account the Ohio River & the great falls." This note appears to be in Nathan Boone's writing]. I don't think that Daniel Boone ever forted on the Yadkin—Daniel Boone was not on either Colonel Montgomeries or Colonel Grants Expaditions against the Cherokees.

5. I do not think that Daniel Boone took any part in the war of the Regulators against Governor Tryon of N. Carolina.

6. The Boone family settled in North Carolina 1752 when Daniel past most of his time in the woods hunting not only because he fancied that kind of Roving but he made it somewhat profitable as Deer skins and furs were very valuable at that time. In the Spring of 1756 he married Rebecca Bryan, daughter of Joseph Bryan of the Yadkin—settled a small farm on the Yadkin where he Remained for some years, Still following his favorite Persuits hunting. The fall of 1767 he and one William Hill crossed the Mountain with the intention of Seeing the Ohio River. They fell on the Big Sandy and knowing from its cours that it must Run into the Ohio thay continued down it as thay supposed one hundred miles whare they ware Ketched in a Snow Storm and had to Remain the Winter (here he saw the first Buffalow) in the Spring thay Returned to the Yadkin without accomplishing their object—nor did he know for some years afterward what River they had wintered on.

In Summer of 1768 or [ink blot] he made a trip to Florida in comany with three other men William Hill and Houghton [?] the third man's name not Recollected. The object was to explore the countary, they visited Pensacola and traveled a few days journey up the St. Jons River but not liking the countary Returned that fall.

I am not Certain that this is the pricise date of his Florida trip.

7. I never heard Daniel Boone was of any trip cross the mountains except the one above mentioned nor did he come out with a large party of explorers previous to his long hunt.

8. I am unable to state whare Finley was from, but I am inclined to believe that Finley was the man that gave him the information of the Ohio River when on Braddock's Campaign in '55 and that he was not a French man but an Englishman. When Finley and my father met (as I believe a second time) in 1768 he Finley told my father that there must be a better way a cross the mountains than the one he had attempted to

go as the Cherokee Indians frequently went to war against the Northern Indians; thay then made an agreement to raise a small party and make an attempt to cross the mountains further to the westward—Finley describing the Ohio River as knowing something of it did not appear to know the interior of the Countary.

9. I can not describe my father's Station Camp in Kentucky in 1769 & 70 precisely. It was on the Right or near the right bank of the Kentucky River and near the mouth of Red River. I don't Recollect of ever hearing him say that he camped in a Rockhouse near Harrodsburgh—it may be so; for it is a very common thing for hunters to do so. Whilst left alone he did not Remain at what thay called their Station Camp, and seldom staid two nights in a place after Stuart left him he didn't hunt game as he had very little ammunition, but explored the countary as low down as the falls of Ohio, the object of Stuart's Returning to North Carolina was for ammunition as thay had lost all by the Indians finding their Station Camp while absent on a Reconitering tour I think it was in the latter part of the year 1769 whilst on this Reconituring Tour that the Indians stole my father & Stuart's horses thay followed the Indians two days, and at night sole from the Indians some of their horses; the Indians, in turn, persued them and made them both prisoners, Kept them in confinement two days when they made their Escape by Jumping into a Canebrake while the Indians were gathering wood to kindle a fire on their return to their Station Camp thay found the camp plundered of everything in making their esape that evening my father got holt of a Indian gun in stead of his own and which was of but little use though he could make out to kill his meat with it.

I think it was at this Station Camp whare Finley and party Separated from my father Shortly after they had established it as a Station Camp. Finley, Mooney and two or three others went on to Green River to hunt and trap My father met with Finley afterwards either on the Green River or the Big Barren. Wheather this was before or after Squire Boone joined him or not I am unable to say.

10. I allways understood my father to say that only one man accompanied Squire Boone in 1770 I think he was by the name of Neely, and he returned in a short time to N. Carolina alone. Jesse Boone didn't accompany Squire Boone—he lived and died in North Carolina.

11. My father nor party ware not employed to explore Kentucky in

1769 or 70 but my father was imployed by Henderson & Co. in 1774-75 and afterwards.

12. John Stuart parted with my father shortly after they had made their escape from the Indians; he was to return at a Certain Time they ware to meet at a certain Camp (not their Station Camp) but lower down the Kentucky River I think where they were then encamped. My father Rambled a bout over the Countary during which time he found several of the Salt Springs which in every Case was Easily found by the large Buffalow Roads leading to them. I think it was while a lone that he visited the upper & lower Blue Licks & the Falls of Ohio before the time appointed to meet Stuart in the neighbourhood of their old Station Camp whare he loitered about untill the appointed time to meet Stuart the place appointed to meet was on the Right bank of the Kentucky River he went to the place appointed; he found nothing their being a very rainy time and the River very high; he supposed that Stuart might be on the opposite side of the River. In a few days the River got within its banks when my father Crossed and found where a fire had been made a few days previous and in looking Round found the two first Letters of Stuarts name cut on a tree.

About one Month after Stuart parted with my father Squire Boone and Neely met with my father) nothing more was known a bout Stuart untill the Spring of 1775 when my Father and party were marking out a Road; they Reached within a few miles of the Kentucky River. After takin up Camp one of the party discovered the bones of a Man in a hollow tree, thay found Stuart's powder horn lying a mongst the bones My father recognized the horn; it allso had Stuart's name cut on it. On examining the bones they found one of the arm bones broken and the mark of Lead on it My father came to the conclusion that Stuart had been wounded at the place appointed whare they ware to meet.

13. My father had no stated place of incampment after Stuart and Squire Boone Left but Rambled over a great deal of the countary. I never heard my father speak of escaping Captivity by jumping down a precipice—nor escaping by throwing tobacco in the Indians eyes.

14. I canot say what became of any of my fathers early Companions Except Mooney, I understood that he was Killed at the Battle of 74 at the mouth of the Great Kanhaway.

15. They visited Green River I think in '71 and met what is calld the Long hunters—I Canot Say anything as to their meeting.

16. I have heard my Father speak of being Robed by the indians while himself and Stuart ware together & again while Squire Boone and himself ware alone the particulars I Canot relate.

17. In 1773 when my Father set out for Kentucky with his famaly there was a Mr. William Russell who agreed to join him on the way with a small party of emigrants. James Boone my Brother was sent by Russells to inform him of my father's departure, James Boone continued with Russell and party for several days, when thinking themselves within a day's travel of my father on the 9th of October '73, James Boone and Six or Seven other men Left Russell's party with the view of joining my father & party that night. Night overtaken them thay incamped on the bank of Wallens Creek two miles in the Rear of my fathers party—On the morning of the 10th awhile before day thay ware fell on by a party of indians, James Boone young Henry Russell and four others war Killed—the names of the Latter four not Recollected—James Boone was in his 17th year when he was Killed.

Nathan Boone

APPENDIX B

Family Genealogy

Boone Family Record copied by L.C. Draper during a visit to Nathan Boone, Sept. & Oct. 1851.

Births

Daniel Boone, Senior, was born October 22d 1734 .
Rebecca Bryan, wife of Daniel Boone, was born Feb. 7th 1739.
James Boone, son of Daniel & Rebecca Boone, was born May 3d 1757.
Israel Boone, son of Daniel & Rebecca Boone, was born January 25th 1759.
Susannah Boone, daughter of Daniel and Rebecca Boone, was born November 2d, 1760.
Jemima Boone, daughter of Daniel & Rebecca Boone, was born October 4th 1762.
Levina Boone, daughter of Daniel & Rebecca Boone, was born March 23, 1766.[1]
Daniel Morgan Boone, son of Daniel & Rebecca Boone, was born May 26th 1768.
Rebecca Boone, daughter of Daniel & Rebecca Boone, was born _____.[2]
Jesse Bryan Boone, son of Daniel & Rebecca Boone, was born in 1773.
William Boone, son of Daniel & Rebecca Boone was born _____.[3]
Nathan Boone, son of Daniel & Rebecca Boone, was born in Boone's Station, Fayette Co., Kentucky, March 2, 1781.

Deaths

Daniel Boone, Sr. died in St. Charles Co., Mo. Sept. 26th 1820, aged 85 years, eleven months & 4 days.

Rebecca, wife of Daniel Boone, Sr., died in St. Charles Co., Mo., March 18th 1813, aged 74 years, 1 month & 11 days.

James Boone, son of Daniel & Rebecca Boone, was killed by the Shawnese Indians, when crossing the Clinch Mountains in Virginia, October 10th, 1773, aged 16 years, 5 months and 7 days.

Israel Boone, son of Daniel and Rebecca Boone, was killed at the battle of the Blue Licks, in Kentucky, August 19th 1782, aged 23 years, 6 months & 25 days.

Susannah Boone, daughter of Daniel and Rebecca Boone, and wife of Wm. Hays, died in what is now St. Charles county, Mo., Oct. 19th, 1800, aged 39 years, 11 months & 27 days.

Jemima Boone, daughter of Daniel and Rebecca Boone, and wife of Flanders Callaway, died in Montgomery County, Missouri.[4]

Levina Boone, daughter of Danl & Rebecca Boone, & wife of Joseph Scholl, died in Clark Co., Kentucky Apl 6th, 1802, aged 36 years & 15 days.

Daniel Morgan Boone, son of Danl & Rebecca Boone, died in Jackson County, Mo. July 13th 1839, aged 71 years, one month and 19 days.

Rebecca Boone, daughter of Danl & Rebecca Boone, wife of Philip Goe, died in Clark Co. Ky _____.

Jesse Bryan Boone, son of Daniel & Rebecca Boone, died in St. Louis, Mo., while a member of the 1st Legislature of the State of Missouri.

William Boone, son of Danl & Rebecca Boone died {in infancy on Clinch & in 1775}.

I certify that the above is a correct copy of the Family Record, a portion of which is in my father, Col. Danl. Boone's handwriting—carefully copied from the original—which original is now partly mutilated & is herewith presented to Lyman C. Draper.

Ash Grove, Green Co., Mo. Nov. 4th 1851.
Nathan Boone.

Notes

1. His Early Life

1. Squire Boone Sr. came to America in 1713 with a broth[

2. Note by Draper: "See Daniel Bryan's statement taken by Shane," Draper Manuscript (hereafter DM) 22C14.

3. Note by Draper: "Incident of Boone & Miller in Judge N notes." (The Nathan Boone interview is file 6S of the Draper Draper's notes are intermixed with the text, written between the li in the margins of the pages. I do not cite specific reference numb notes when I quote from them. My notes make reference also to Manuscript files, however, such as that for Draper's interview with I and in those cases reference numbers are supplied.)

4. During the French and Indian War, General Edward B the commander of the army that attempted to recapture Fort Duc present site of Pittsburgh. Colonel George Washington served und and commanded the Virginia militia. On July 9, 1755, when only from the French fort, the British and American army of fifteen h was defeated by three hundred French and Indians. Braddock v wounded during the battle.

5. Colonel William Byrd, a prominent Virginian, was orde 1760 to rescue the men at Fort Loudoun, who were besieged by the Byrd did not act promptly, and the fort surrendered on August 7.

John Montgomery (1748-1794) was born in Botetourt Coun He served as an officer under Colonel William Byrd in the Cheroke of 1760-1761, under Colonel William Preston during Dunmore under Colonel William Christian during the Cherokee campaign 1778 he was a company commander under Colonel George Roge Illinois and in 1779 was on another campaign against the Cheroke command of Colonel Isaac Shelby. Later Montgomery moved to then Tennessee, and was the founder of Clarksville, Tennessee. See I

Major James Grant was in command of a detachment under General hn Forbes, who led an ill-fated scouting expedition from Loyalhanna toward rt Duquesne in October 1758. The Virginia militia units in this expedition re commanded by Colonel Andrew Lewis and Captain James Byrd. This mbined force was defeated by the French and Indians. Afterward he was sent South Carolina for a campaign against the Cherokee. While Byrd was camped the Holston, Grant continued to press the Cherokee, and by 1761 he de- ited them and destroyed fifteen of their towns.

6. Draper is referring to John Haywood, author of *The Civil and Political story of the State of Tennessee from Its Earliest Settlement up to the Year 1796; cluding the Boundaries of the State* (Knoxville, Tenn., 1823) and *The Natural d Aboriginal History of Tennessee up to the First Settlement Therein by the White ople in the Year 1768* (Nashville, Tenn., 1823).

7. Fort Dobbs was located about twenty miles east of the Boone home- ad, between the south fork of the Yadkin River and the Catawba River, near e present town of Statesville, North Carolina. Lyman Draper believed that ring the Indian trouble in 1759 the Boone family moved to Virginia or Mary- d instead of seeking protection at this fort. See DM 2C169-70.

8. John Finley (or Findley) was born in northern Ireland in 1722 and at early age was brought to Pennsylvania by his parents. In 1744, at the age of enty-two, he was licensed as a trader and the same year married Elizabeth arris. In 1775 he left Lancaster, Pennsylvania, on a western trading mission d never returned. Lucien Beckner, "John Findley: The First Pathfinder," *Filson ub History Quarterly* 43 (July 1969):206-15. According to John Mack Faragher, *niel Boone, The Life and Legend of an American Pioneer* (New York, 1992), his t trading mission began in 1772.

9. Although Jack and William Blevins, Elisha Walden, and Henry Skaggs re all early long hunters on the Cumberland River, it was probably a party led Kasper Mansker who discovered Daniel Boone in 1770 lying on his back ging. See Faragher, *Boone*, p. 85; DM 32S481, interview with George Smith, 44; and DM 31C60.

10. This refers to a legend that Daniel Boone nearly shot Rebecca while nting deer at night with a torch. See Faragher, *Boone*, p. 43, and John Bakeless, *niel Boone* (New York, 1939), p. 27.

11. This chapter is from DM 6S18-43.

2. The Hunter

1. John Filson, *The Discovery, Settlement and present State of Kentucke* Vilmington, Del., 1784), p. 51, and Daniel Bryan, DM 22C14, both give the te of their capture as December 22, 1769.

2. Marginal note by Draper: "See Croghan's journal. The Shawnees dur- ; the French War left the mouth of Scioto, and went and settled at the Scioto

Plains—and there they resided till after the War of 1774. In 1778 the most of them seem to have been located at the Little Miami and some on Paint Creek of Scioto. For the Warrior's Path, compare Gov. Pownall and Filsons maps and Hutchins."

3. Daniel Bryan, DM 22C14.

4. Marginal note by Draper: "I am now satisfied Jesse Boone did visit Kentucky in 1770: see T. C. Land's letters, Sept. 28 and Oct. 1885." His correspondence with T.C. Land can be found in DM 19C.

5. The old Station Camp was on Station Camp Creek, a branch of the Kentucky River near Irvine, Kentucky. The Red River empties into the Kentucky River about fourteen miles downstream of Station Camp Creek and about nine miles west of Boonesboro. In 1775 Stewart's body was located on a section of Boone's trace, which went down Otter Creek to Boonesboro.

6. Draper added as a note that he subsequently visited an aged son of Mrs. Pennington near Macomb, Illinois. In DM 4C99 there is a lengthy list of Stewart's and Pennington's descendants and their addresses.

Stewart is an old English name sometimes found in Scotland. Draper was casual in spelling Stewart's name and also used "Stuart." The name is spelled "Stewart" by Filson but "Stuart" by Bakeless.

7. The Falls of the Ohio is located at present-day Louisville, Kentucky.

8. Daniel Bryan, DM 22C14.

9. This hunter was Zachariah Green, and the incident occurred at the "Three Forks" of the Cumberland River, probably near Somerset, Kentucky. See DM 32S526. This paragraph was moved from DM 6S285.

10. This paragraph is from DM 6S84.

11. See note 6, chapter 1.

12. This chapter is from DM 6S44-78 except for paragraphs cited in notes 9 and 10.

3. To Kentucky

1. Henry Russell, the son of William Russell, was also wounded and later killed by the Indians. This incident occurred along what is now U.S. Highway 68, about five miles east of Jonesville, Virginia. They were then about forty miles west of Castlewood. For a complete account see James William Hagy, "The First Attempt to Settle Kentucky: Boone in Virginia," *Filson Club History Quarterly* 53 (July 1979): 227-33. William Russell (c. 1738-1793), the son of William Russell Sr., was born in Culpepper County and attended William and Mary College. In 1769 he moved to the frontier and established a station called Castlewood. He led an active military life. He fought in the battle of Point Pleasant and later under General George Washington fought in battles at Brandywine, Germantown, and Monmouth. He was eventually commissioned a brigadier general. This William Russell had a son named William Russell,

who is subsequently mentioned in this book. DM 5B35-40. Draper note: "See American Archives, 1774, folio 873. Col. Ar. Campbell's letter, Oct 16, 1774, in Preston Papers, vol. iii, shows one of the Cherokee murderers was killed by that nation."

2. Draper note: "and perhaps to collect the cattle scattered."

3. Both John Gass and David Gass were early settlers at Boonesboro. For Draper's correspondence with John Gass, see DM 24C.

4. Draper's note in the top margin of this page reads: "References: Edinburgh Advertiser 1774, p. 147-48."

5. Michael Stoner (or Holsteiner) was a long hunter from Virginia who was selected to accompany Boone on this mission to Kentucky in 1774. In 1775 he was hired by Richard Henderson as a hunter for the Transylvania Company, stayed in Kentucky, and was awarded land on Stoner's Fork of the Licking River (near Daniel Boone's original land claim) but sold this tract to Henry Clay. He was wounded in the wrist during the attack on Boonesboro in 1777. He was still alive in 1816 and resided in Wayne County, Kentucky. See DM 4C130.

6. It is more likely that Daniel Boone encountered the survivors of Hancock Taylor's surveying party somewhere south of present-day Richmond, Kentucky, perhaps at Roundstone Lick or one of the smaller licks farther south. He did not find the surveying party of John Floyd or the one led by James Douglas and Isaac Hite.

7. This "buffalo dung" may still be seen attached to the limestone rock outcrops at the falls. It is a black fossil.

8. For information on this trip, see two articles by Neal Hammon that appeared in the *Filson Club History Quarterly*: "Legend of Daniel Boone's Cabin at Harrodsburg," 48 (July 1974): 241-52, and "John Filson's Error," 59 (Oct. 1985): 462.

9. Draper note: "See Shane Papers, Vol 1, Jessamine Co., p. 10-11." In a second note Draper also cites "William Russell's letter of Aug. 28, 1774 and Arthur Campbell's letter of same date found in Preston Papers, Vol. iii." For additional information on Boone's service on the Clinch River, see Major Arthur Campbell to Colonel William Preston, Sept. 29 and Oct. 12, 1774, DM 3QQ106 and DM 3QQ118, and Captain Daniel Smith to Colonel William Prestion, Oct. 13, 1774, DM 3QQ115.

10. John McKinney was in Colonel Lewis's division; see Reuben Gold Thwaites and Louise Phelps Kellogg, *Documentary History of Dunmore's War, 1774* (Madison, Wis., 1905), p. 422. The above two paragraphs have been moved from DM 6S286.

11. For additional information on the Transylvania Company, see George W. Ranck, *Boonesborough* (Louisville, Ky., 1901), and Archibald Henderson, "Transylvania Company Personnel," *Filson Club History Quarterly* 21 (Jan. 1947): 3-21.

12. Draper note: "see Hening vii, 214."

13. This lick was located at present-day Nashville, Tennessee.

14. Fort Boone was on the banks of the Kentucky River, a few hundred feet downstream from the main fort at Boonesboro, at the site of the existing public restrooms in Boonesboro State Park. This little fort was burned by Indians in 1777. Susannah Hays was a daughter of Daniel Boone.

15. Simon Kenton (1755-1836) was born in Fauquier County, Virginia, and as a young man became a frontier hunter and explorer. In 1775 he moved to Kentucky and lived in both Boonesboro and Harrodsburg. During the attack on Boonesboro in 1777, he carried the wounded Daniel Boone back to the fort. He served under Colonel George Rogers Clark in Illinois. While stealing horses in Ohio, he was captured by Indians but escaped and returned to Kentucky. In 1784 he built Kenton's Station in Mason County but later moved to Ohio.

16. Betsy (Elizabeth) and Frances Callaway, daughters of Colonel Richard Callaway. Their capture occurred on the Kentucky River near Boonesboro, and they were rescued on Flatt Creek, in what is now Bath County, Kentucky. See John Floyd to William Preston, July 21, 1776, DM 4C20 and DM 33S300. Elizabeth married Samuel Henderson, the brother of Colonel Richard Henderson, and Frances married John Holder.

17. Matthew Arbuckle was near the Shawnee town when this party of Indians returned, and he reported that two of the kidnappers had been killed during the rescue. See letter of Matthew Arbuckle to Colonel William Fleming, Fort Randolph, Aug. 15, 1776, DM 7C17(2).

Draper's note says that "according to his statement in Hunt's Review, dictated by Maj. Smith, who there claims to have killed one of the Indians—hence I infer he must have shot, and I think was the one mentioned by Maj. Reid and intimated in the Wester Review article—was Smith, who was a boasting character. The Westn Review article claims that McMillan made one of the shots. It must be that Reid's Indian information relative to where the Indian sentinel was is incorrect. That from all the statements the sentinel must have gone down to the fire—doubtless to light his pipe, as the fire was just started—and perhaps to see what progress was making in cooking the meat. Unless the sentinel did leave his post and leave his gun there, the girls would not have known of his gun having been left there, as Capt. Gass states."

18. Goodman had been a companion of Daniel Boone on hunting and scouting expeditions in 1775-1776. In 1795 Daniel Boone testified for Goodman's heirs in a land suit. See Shelby County Deed Book 1, p. 272, Shelbyville, Ky.

19. Some historians also include the statement that Simon Kenton assisted Boone in making his escape.

20. This chapter is from DM 6S79-102.

4. Captured by Indians

1. In 1778, February 7 was on Saturday.

2. Mays Lick is near U.S. Highway 68 in Mason County, Kentucky, about ten miles from the Ohio River and about ten miles from the Lower Blue Licks.

3. This paragraph is from DM 6S282.

4. If Boone had been captured in the vicinity of Mays Lick, the Indians must have crossed the river and circled around to the south to prevent the salt makers from escaping. There were two salt springs near the river, the one on the north side being the largest.

5. Joseph Jackson (1755-1845) was born in Bedford County, Virginia, and went to Kentucky in Captain Watkins's company in the fall of 1777. He lived in both Missouri and Bourbon County, Kentucky. He was personally interviewed by Lyman Draper in 1844. See DM 11C.

6. See John D. Barnhart, *Henry Hamilton and George Rogers Clark in the American Revolution* (Crawfordsville, Ind., 1951).

7. The Huron River is probably what is now called the Sandusky River. Its headwaters are not far from those of the Miami and Scioto Rivers. Huron Indians lived in this region.

8. Andrew Johnson was later awarded 1,400 acres of land on Cartwright Creek in Kentucky.

9. Both were captured with the salt makers at the Blue Licks. James Brooks (1761-1816) was later awarded 1,400 acres of land on Silver Creek in Kentucky but died a poor man. James Callaway was the brother of Flanders and Micajah Callaway. He eventually escaped and returned to Kentucky. He later moved to Missouri, where he died in 1835.

10. Micajah Callaway apparently adopted Indian ways but was released in 1783, later serving as a scout for General "Mad" Anthony Wayne. He was awarded a Spanish land grant in Missouri, located just east of where his brother Flanders lived. He died in 1849.

11. Jesse Copher, from Culpepper County, Virginia, escaped with Nathaniel Bullock and Simon Kenton in June 1779. See DM 4B199. He married a niece of Daniel Boone and died in 1822.

12. Nathaniel Bullock (1737-1820) was born in Virginia. He escaped with Kenton and Copher and returned to Kentucky, where he married the Widow Boughman (or Boofman). For Draper's interview with Bullock, see DM 23C.

13. William Hancock (1738-1821) was born in Goochland County, Virginia, and served in the French and Indian War. He escaped from the Indians in time to defend the fort at Boonesboro. In 1782 he was in the Battle of Blue Licks. He received 1,400 acres of land on Otter Creek near Boonesboro. He is said to have moved to Missouri in 1799.

14. Nathan gives a reasonable but not exact quote from Filson, *Discovery, Settlement and present State*, p. 66.

15. This chapter is from DM 6S103-29.

5. Siege of Boonesboro

1. Moses Boone's drawing of the fort (see DM 19C12) would indicate that the walls were extended southward, or in an upriver direction. Two houses and the blacksmith shop, which were presumably along the original wall, were then left freestanding inside the walls.

2. Daniel Boone gives the number as 444 Indians, "commanded by Capt. Duquesne, [with] eleven other Frenchmen." Filson, *Discovery, Settlement and present State*, p. 68.

3. Squire Boone was wounded at the outset of this siege, so Colonel Richard Callaway was the man who fired the wooden cannon. See Chester Raymond Young, ed., *Westward into Kentucky: The Narrative of Daniel Trabue* (Lexington, Ky., 1981), p. 58.

4. The Indians' tunnel began at the riverbank and went westward to undermine the fort near the northeast blockhouse. For the location of the countertunnel, see Moses Boone's sketch.

5. Draper note: "This tomahawking and beheading operation is a mistake from Capt. Gass and Moses Boone's recollections."

6. Draper note: "This was certainly not Black Fish or if it was, the incident happened on Bowman's Campaign in the following year."

7. John Mason Peck, *The Life of Daniel Boone* (Boston, 1847).

8. Daniel Boone was tried by court-martial after the attack of Boonesboro but was aquitted and promoted. Allan W. Eckert wrote an entire book on the subject, *The Court Martial of Daniel Boone* (Boston, 1973).

9. One reason Daniel Boone returned to Kentucky was to obtain a certificate of settlement from the Virginia land commissioners. He received this 400 acres for the sum of two pounds and an additional 1,000-acre preemption tract for two hundred pounds, Virginia paper money. His settlement and preemption warrants were on Stoner Fork of the Licking River, east of present-day Winchester, Kentucky. Apparently this site was too exposed and dangerous, and so he chose to settle his new station farther south, on Boone Creek, on land claimed by his son Israel.

10. Draper note: "This was given by Genl. Rutherford and hence Boone must have enjoyed that patriot's fullest confidence—See Danl. Bryan's narrative."

11. Draper note: "Va. Gazette, July 26, 1780, shows this robbery occurred at James City, Va. He later offered to pay Mrs. N. Hart £300 compensation."

12. Jack Dunn escaped from the Indians c. 1778-1779, returned to Ken-

tucky, and later disappeared during the next campaign against the Indian towns. He was then thought to be a turncoat.

13. This statement is incorrect, as both places had acquired their names prior to this event. Boone Creek was where the Indians had captured Daniel Boone c. 1769, and the lick now called Boone's Blue Lick was near present-day Berea, where Boone hunted prior to and during his trip to Kentucky in 1775.

14. Colonel Banastre Tarleton (1754-1833), under orders from General Cornwallis, led the 70 infantrymen of the 23rd British Regiment and 180 dragoons from his legion on a raid toward Charlottesville on June 3, 1781. See Robert D. Bass, *The Green Dragoon* (Columbia, S.C., 1973), pp. 178-79.

15. The traitor Benedict Arnold was in charge of the expedition that invaded Virginia on January 3, 1781, and on June 4 Tarleton advanced against Charlottesville, where he captured and destroyed supplies destined for General Nathanael Greene's army.

16. Captain John [Jack] Jouett (1754-1822) was born in Albemarle County, Virginia. He may have accompanied John Floyd to Kentucky in 1775, where a small creek near Boonesboro was named for him. He was made famous by his ride to Charlottesville to warn Governor Thomas Jefferson of Tarleton's advance. After the war he moved to Kentucky and built a house near Versailles, Kentucky, which may still be visited.

17. This chapter is from DM 6S129-51.

6. Bryan's Station and the Blue Licks Defeat

1. Draper note: "Dec. 13, 1804—See Pioneer Families of Missouri, p. 70."

2. Draper note: "Col. Nathan Boone at first thought he got into the fort, but yields that point." Actually most of the mounted men did reach and take shelter inside the fort. Bryan's Station was located about six miles northeast of Lexington on the main road to the Lower Blue Licks.

3. The two ravines are both on the west side of the trail, so the first depression must be passed to get to the second. There is no ravine on the east side other than the river valley itself.

4. Major Hugh McGary, originally from North Carolina, was an early settler at Harrodsburg. He came to Kentucky with Daniel Boone during Boone's second trip in 1775. A militia officer of Lincoln County, Virginia, his conduct at the battle was later criticized, and he was blamed for the defeat. In 1786, then a lieutenant colonel in the Mercer County militia, he personally executed the captive Indian chief Moluntha with a small ax because he had been at Blue Licks. He eventually moved to Shawneetown, Illinois, where he died in 1808.

5. The left or west wing consisted of a company of militia from Fayette County; the other two companies were commanded by Hugh McGary and Stephen Trigg, both consisting of men from Lincoln County. John Todd was

the overall leader of the expedition. Benjamin Logan was advancing toward Blue Licks with reinforcements. An enemy attack on the right flank broke the lines of Trigg's company, causing a general retreat. Both Todd and Trigg were killed. This battle occurred on August 19, 1782.

6. Colonel Benjamin Logan led an expedition back to the battlefield on August 24, expecting to find the enemy still present.

7. Daniel Boone was correct; the enemy had no more than eleven killed, whereas the American loss was about seventy-five. Alexander McKee to Major De Peyster, August 28, 1782, Colonial Office Records, series 2, vol. 20, p. 288, Reports of the Public Archives of Canada, Canadian Archives, Ottawa.

8. Loramie's Fort was about twenty-five miles north of present-day Greenville, Ohio.

9. Marble Creek is a small creek draining into the Kentucky River, located between Boone Creek and Hickman Creek. The headwaters are about five or six miles southwest of Boone's Station. Draper notes: "See Shane Collection" and "Dec 11, 1782, Fayette County Court, Col. Boone was appointed a Deputy Survey, and he was also in Court on August, 1783."

10. According to Virginia land records, 1,400 acres of land on the headwaters of Marble Creek were originally acquired and patented in the name of William Hays. The survey was dated January 25, 1783, and the patent was in June 1784. Hays had purchased the land from "William Stafford, assee, &c" prior to the time it was surveyed. A smaller tract of 379 acres was claimed and surveyed by William Hays and Daniel Boone on a treasury warrant adjacent to and northwest of Hays's 1,400 acres, which was also bounded by James Shelby's land. The Shelby land was located on the Shelby Fork of Hickman's Creek. The Hays-Boone tract was also surveyed on January 25, 1783, and on July 17 of the same year it was assigned to Boone. In the opinion of the editor, Daniel Boone probably lived on the 379-acre tract, although it would be stretching the facts to say the land was on Marble Creek.

11. Limestone is where Maysville, Kentucky, is now located. It was an early Ohio River landing place for Kentucky settlers. The small creek nearby was also called Limestone.

12. This campaign was against the Ohio Indians. Daniel Boone is listed as a participant on the original pay records. See Military Certificates, photocopy book of original document, no. 976.903/M644i, Kentucky Historical Society, Frankfort, Ky.

13. Draper note: "Captain Irvine."

14. Thomas Ferguson (or Fargison) from Greenbrier, Virginia, was also present at the Battle of Point Pleasant. See Thwaites and Kellogg, *Dunmore's War*, p. 410.

15. The land records prove that Daniel Boone was at Wilson's Station near Harrodsburg on January 17, 1780, so this hunting trip would have been later.

16. Lewis Wetzel (1763-1808) was a well-known West Virginia hunter and Indian fighter. He was the son of John Wetzel, a German, who settled his family on Wheeling Creek in 1772. He was arrested for the murder of an Indian during a time of peace, which is probably the incident mentioned by Nathan Boone.

17. This chapter is from DM 6S151-74.

7. Point Pleasant

1. In 1789 and 1790 a number of people were killed by the Indians while traveling down the Ohio, including John May, the well-known Kentucky land jobber from Petersburg, Virginia, the brother of George May, surveyor of Kentucky and Jefferson Counties. Charles Johnson, John May's assistant, was present and in 1827 published an account of his capture, which was reprinted by Frederick Drimmer (*Captured by the Indians, 15 Firsthand Accounts, 1750-1870* [New York, 1965], pp. 185-218). Although Flinn was burned at the stake, Johnson believed that Skyles was eventually set free and returned home.

About the same time, Lord Dorchester, the Canadian governor, wrote that the Indians were on the warpath. There were fewer than eight hundred regular soldiers in the entire American army then, and only a few were posted on the western frontier.

2. Nathan Boone probably is referring to the town now called Greenup, on the Ohio River at the mouth of the Little Sandy River.

3. Draper note: "It was really in fall of 1791; elected 4th Apl. 1791; and session commenced about Oct. 17th and continued till as late as Dec. 20, 1791."

4. Henry Miller was an old friend of Daniel Boone's; see accounts of their activities in chapter 1. The powder horn mentioned in this paragraph may be the same one presently on display at Nathan Boone's stone house in St. Charles County, Missouri.

5. Present-day St. Albans, West Virginia.

6. This famous leap is reported by many historians with minor variations. It should not be confused with the alleged leap of Major Samuel McCullock near Wheeling, which is said to have occurred in 1777.

7. Nathan is possibly referring to the Flint River.

8. Draper noted the date as 1793.

9. Draper note: "This must have been in the fall of 1789."

10. Chickamauga Creek is about four miles below the mouth of the Kanawha River on the Ohio side.

11. Sixteen Mile Creek is about twelve miles below Chickamauga Creek. Crab Creek is located six miles below Chickamauga Creek.

12. Draper notes that this must have been after May 1794.

13. Colonel Andrew Lewis's old fort, called Fort Blair, was built in 1774 after the Battle of Point Pleasant. In 1775 this fort was abandoned and later

burned by the Indians. In the early summer of 1776, Captain Matthew Arbuckle constructed another fort to replace it, which was called Fort Randolph in honor of Peyton Randolph, a leading Virginia patriot.

14. This chapter is from DM 6S175-204.

8. Back to Kentucky

1. According to this description, the farm would be in the vicinity of present-day Carlisle, Kentucky. Brushy Creek and Brushy Fork are two separate but parallel streams that flow into Hinkston Creek in the vicinity of Millersburg. The main buffalo trace leading to the Lower Blue Lick went along Brushy Creek.

2. Greasy Creek flows into the Sandy River on the west side; there is a small community still called Boons Camp on this creek about five miles west of what is now Paintsville in Johnson County, Kentucky. The Burning Spring was on the headwaters of the Licking River, near the Floyd-Magoffin county line, which is west of present-day Salyersville.

3. Andrew Hood had moved to Kentucky and established Hood's Station by 1785 according to DM 11CC85 and DM 14U. The station was said to be in what is now Clark County.

4. The headwaters of Grassy Lick Creek are about ten miles northeast of Winchester, Kentucky, and about forty miles south of Limestone (now Maysville).

5. Blaine Creek is a branch of the Big Sandy River that flows through Lawrence County, Kentucky. It is south of the headwaters of the Little Sandy River.

6. This chapter is from DM 6S205-12.

9. To Missouri

1. An arpent is equivalent to 0.8507 acres.

2. George Buchanan is later mentioned as the young man who assisted Daniel Boone in driving livestock to Missouri.

3. The author has located fourteen depositions of Daniel Boone, taken between 1794 and 1817; another was probably destroyed when the Scott County, Kentucky, courthouse burned.

4. This statement seems to be an exaggeration, as Virginia and Kentucky records show only 28,088 acres of land claimed by Daniel Boone, sometimes in partnership with William Hays. Most tracts were sold before Boone received any grants for the land.

5. Green Clay (1757-1826) was born in Virginia and moved to Madison

County, Kentucky, c. 1781. He served in the legislature and led volunteer troops during the War of 1812. He was a second cousin of Henry Clay.

6. Daniel Boone's surveys were not limited to simple rectangles. He also made some complicated surveys with multiple sides running in various directions. For examples see Virginia surveys nos. 1069, 1070, 2371, 2886; Dept. of State, Frankfort, Ky.

7. According to Ken Kemper, the historian of the Daniel Boone and Frontier Families Research Association, there is no record of any person named Flanders Callaway Jr. He believes that this entry was a mistake in the Nathan Boone/Lyman Draper transfer of information. The sixteen-year-old second son was in fact James Callaway, who is mentioned later in this interview.

8. The Cuivre River reaches the Mississippi about twenty miles north of St. Charles, Missouri. This manuscript uses the spelling "Quivre."

9. About twenty-five miles west of St. Charles.

10. Olive Boone also described the trip to Missouri as follows: "After the death of my father, Peter Van Bibber, my mother and I lived with my brother in Ohio, on the Ohio, opposite the mouth of the Big Sandy River. I was married on the 26th of Sept., 1799. On the first of October, without any company but my husband, I started to Missouri, or Upper Louisiana. We had two ponies and our packhorse. After being on our journey some time we were overtaken by a man and woman who travelled with us to Vincennes. We remained there nearly three weeks, in consequence of getting one of our ponies crippled. We traveled along the remainder of the way, arriving in St. Louis the last of October. My husband was offered eighty acres of land (in the center of what was afterwards the city) for one of our ponies. He laughed and said he would not give one of the ponies for the whole town. We went to St. Charles County, and located about twenty miles above St. Charles. We crossed the Missouri River at St. Charles by placing our goods in a skiff. My husband rowed and I steered and held the horse by the bridle. It was rather a perilous trip for so young a couple. I was just sixteen, my husband eighteen." Hazel Atterbury Spraker, *The Boone Family, a Genealogical History of the Descendants of George and Mary Boone Who Came to America in 1717* (Baltimore, 1977), p. 121.

11. Daniel M. Boone's grant was near the village of Matson, Missouri, on the ridge overlooking the Missouri River. Daniel Boone Sr. had an adjacent land grant to the east extending to the river, and Isaac Van Bibber and William Hays had grants to the northeast.

12. Draper marginal note: "For an account of Femme Osage Settlement see Stoddard's Louisiana, p 222; Pecks Gazette." Stoddard was the U.S. delegate appointed to be in charge of Missouri in 1904, when the French lost control of the area.

13. The grant purchased by Nathan Boone was located along County Road F, about four miles south of New Melle, Missouri.

14. Loutre River is in Montgomery County, Missouri, about forty miles

west or upriver from Nathan Boone's home, and the Loutre Lick is on the headwaters, near Danville in Franklin County, Missouri.

15. James Mackey was the Spanish commandant of this district, called St. Andre del Missionary.

16. This paragraph is from DM 6S281-82.

17. At this time John Coburn, originally from Philadelphia, was the judge of the Superior Court for the Territory of Louisiana.

18. Daniel Boone had surveyed Bridges's settlement and preemption claim of 1,400 acres on Muddy Creek in 1783. Bridges was one of the settlers who had come to Kentucky with Boone in 1775.

19. This chapter is from DM 6S213-26.

10. Hunting in Missouri

1. Isaac Van Bibber had a tavern near the lick. Loutre Lick was on the headwaters of what is now called the Loutre River, not on the Bourbeuse River. This was the site of the original Spanish land grant of Nathan Boone.

2. Florissant is now a suburb of St. Louis.

3. The Osage River meets the Missouri River just east of Fort Jefferson; the headwaters are in Kansas. The Niangua River has its headwaters north of Springfield, Missouri, and joins the Osage in the existing Lake of the Ozarks.

4. Draper note: "Rogerstown on the Merrimack River, is noted on map of Missouri in Westmore's Gazt."

5. Probably the Grand River, which is a branch of the Osage River, located in the vicinity of Clinton, Missouri. There is another Grand River north of the Missouri River near Chillicothe. The Pomme de Terre is a tributary of Grand River that flows southward toward Springfield, Missouri.

6. A capote is a coat with a hood, frequently worn by French Canadians during this period.

7. Now usually spelled Niangua.

8. Rocheport is ten miles west of Columbia on the Missouri River.

9. This large, handsome, and obviously expensive stone house on Nathan's grant is open to visitors. The tour guides claim that the masonry work was done by Nathan and the woodwork by his father, Daniel Boone. However, the workmanship would suggest that it was built by very skilled craftsmen with years of experience in their respective trades. Also, according to this text, Daniel Boone worked as a blacksmith during the time he lived on this property.

10. Boone's Lick is near the Missouri River, about ten miles west of Fayette in Howard County, Missouri.

11. Draper notes say this date was too early, and the year should have been September 1808. This paragraph is from DM 6S289-90.

12. The Lamine River is southwest of Booneville, and the Kansas River

joins the Missouri River at Kansas City. When they met the Indian they had already traveled 180 miles from home.

13. Draper note: "Sni-a-bar is one of the names, so common in Missouri and Illinois, manufactured by the old pioneers out of Indian, French and German. This word is partly French and partly German. The first syllable is from the French word chenal—canal, channel, or slough. The latter part is a memorial of an old German trapper, who, in ascending the river with his canoe in high water, entered this creek, supposing it a channel or 'cut-off' behind an island, and didn't find out his mistake until he got to the prairie. His name was Aber, and the French voyageurs named the creek Chenal Aber, out of which the American pioneers made the name Sni-a-bar."

14. Draper note: "The country records at Fulton, show that Mr. Wm. Hays' will bears date March 12, 1845, and was proved the 12th of the succeeding May."

15. This chapter is from DM 6S213-26.

11. The War of 1812

1. Colonel William Russell was then in command of the 7th Infantry Regiment in the regular army. This was the son of William Russell, who attempted to settle in Kentucky with Daniel Boone in 1773. See John E. Kleber, ed., *The Kentucky Encylopedia* (Lexington, Ky., 1992), p. 788.

2. This paragraph is from DM 6S291.

3. Fort Mason would have been between Hannibal and Louisiana, Missouri, or about fifty miles above St. Charles. Colonel Benjamin Howard became the military commander of the Missouri Territory in 1814, but because of illness the duty was assumed by Major Zachary Taylor.

4. The Rock River begins above Rockford, Illinois, and runs into the Mississippi at Rock Island.

5. Draper note: "Colonel Boone thinks what follows transpired in 1812 or early in 1813—but McAfee, Beck's Gazt and Wetmore, say in spring of 1814."

On July 19, 1814, Fort Shelby at Prairie du Chien was surrendered to the British by Lieutenant Joseph Perkins. On the same day Lieutenant John Campbell's force was defeated by the Indians near what is now Rockford, Illinois. These defeats resulted in the offensive action by Major Zachary Taylor. Prairie du Chien is in southwestern Wisconsin at the mouth of the Wisconsin River.

6. Zachary Taylor (1784-1850), a career army officer and hero during the Mexican War, was later the twelfth president of the United States.

7. This paragraph is from DM 6S287-88; the remainder of the chapter is from DM 6S254-67.

12. The Last Years

1. This farm adjoined Charette Creek, but the house and cemetery were near the adjacent Tugue Creek.

2. This chapter is from DM 6S268-81.

Appendix B

1. Draper note: "See the original page 17th, which says March 23d—LCD." This number had been 28 and was corrected to 23.

2. The blank was filled in with the words "abt. early 1770" in Lyman Draper's handwriting.

3. In Draper's writing: "(June or July 1775—died in infancy)."

4. No date given.

BIBLIOGRAPHY

Books

Abernethy, Thomas Perkins. *Western Lands and the American Revolution*. New York, 1937.

Adams, James Truslow, ed. *Atlas of American History*. New York, 1943.

Allen, William B. *A History of Kentucky*. Louisville, Ky., 1872.

Bakeless, John. *Daniel Boone*. New York, 1939.

———. *Turncoats, Traitors, and Heroes*. Philadelphia, 1959.

Barnhart, John D. *Henry Hamilton and George Rogers Clark in the American Revolution*. Crawfordsville, Ind., 1951.

Bass, Robert D. *The Green Dragoon*. Columbia, S.C., 1973.

Bentley, James R. Preface to *Early Kentucky Settlers: The Records of Jefferson County, Kentucky*. Baltimore, 1988. Reprinted from *Filson Club History Quarterly*.

Bodley, Temple. *History of Kentucky*. Vol 1. Louisville, Ky., 1928.

———. *Our First Great West*. Louisville, Ky., 1938.

Bogart, W.H. *Daniel Boone and the Hunters of Kentucky*. Buffalo, N.Y., 1855.

Brawley, James S. *The Rowan Story, 1753-1953: A Narrative History of Rowan County, North Carolina*. Salisbury, N.C., 1953.

Brookes-Smith, Joan E. *Master Index, Virginia Surveys and Grants, 1774-1791*. Frankfort, Ky., 1976.

Butler, Mann. *Valley of the Ohio*. Edited by G. Glenn Clift and Hambleton Tapp. Frankfort, Ky., 1971.

Chief of Engineers of the United States Army. *The Ohio River*. 5th ed. Washington, D.C., 1935.

Chinn, George Morgan. *Kentucky: Settlement and Statehood*. Frankfort, Ky., 1975.

Clark, Jerry E. *The Shawnee*. Lexington, Ky., 1977.

Clark, Thomas D. *Frontier America*. New York, 1959.

———. *A History of Kentucky*. Lexington, Ky., 1954.

Clift, G. Glenn. *Kentucky in Retrospect*. Frankfort, Ky., 1967.

Collins, Lewis. *History of Kentucky*. Cincinnati, Ohio, 1847.

————. *History of Kentucky*. Edited and revised by Richard H.Collins. Louisville, Ky., 1877.

Cook, Michael L., and Bettie Cummings Cook. *Fayette County, Kentucky, Records*. 2 vols. Evansville, Ind., 1985.

Cotterill, R.S. *History of Pioneer Kentucky*. Cincinnati, Ohio, 1917.

Crumrine, Boyd. *Virginia Court Records in Southwestern Pennsylvania*. Baltimore, 1974.

Drimmer, Frederick, ed. *Captured by the Indians, 15 Firsthand Accounts, 1750-1870*. New York, 1965.

Eckert, Allan W. *The Court Martial of Daniel Boone*. Boston, 1973.

————. *The Frontiersman: A Narrative*. Boston, 1967.

Elliott, Lawrence. *The Long Hunter: A New Life of Daniel Boone*. New York, 1976.

Faragher, John Mack. *Daniel Boone: The Life and Legend of an American Pioneer*. New York, 1992.

Filson, John. *The Discovery, Settlement and present State of Kentucke*. Wilmington, Del., 1784.

Flexner, James Thomas. *George Washington and the New Nation*. 4 vols. Boston, 1965-72.

Flint, Timothy. *Biographical Memoir of Daniel Boone, the First Settler of Kentucky*. Philadelphia, 1833.

Ford, Carol Lee, indexer. *Early Kentucky Tax Records*. Baltimore, 1987.

Gwathmey, John H. *Twelve Virginia Counties: Where the Western Migration Began*. Richmond, Va., 1937.

Hamilton, Edward P. *The French and Indian Wars*. New York, 1962.

Hamilton, Holman. *Zachary Taylor: Soldier of the Republic*. Indianapolis, 1941.

Hammon, Neal O. *Early Kentucky Land Records, 1773-1780*. Louisville, Ky., 1992.

Harding, Margery Heberling, comp. *George Rogers Clark and His Men: Military Records, 1778-1784*. Frankfort, Ky., 1981.

Harper, Josephine L., ed. *Guide to the Draper Manuscripts*. Madison, Wis., 1983.

Harrison, Henry. *Surnames of the United Kingdom: A Concise Etymological Dictionary*. 2 vols. London, 1912.

Harrison, Lowell H., and James C. Klotter. *A New History of Kentucky*. Lexington, Ky., 1997.

Haywood, John. *The Civil and Political History of the State of Tennessee from Its Earliest Settlement up to the Year 1796; Including the Boundaries of the State*. Knoxville, Tenn., 1823.

————. *The Natural and Aboriginal History of Tennessee up to the First Settlement Therein by the White People in the Year 1768*. Nashville, Tenn., 1823.

Imlay, Gilbert. *Topographical Description of the Western Territory of North America*. London, 1793.

Isaac, Rhys. *The Transformation of Virginia*. Chapel Hill, N.C., 1982.

James, James Alton. *George Rogers Clark Papers, 1781-1784.* Springfield, Ill., 1924.

Jillson, Willard Rouse. *The Boone Narrative.* Louisville, Ky., 1932.

———. *Pioneer Kentucky.* Frankfort, Ky., 1934.

Johnson, Patricia Givens. *James Patton and the Appalachian Colonist.* Verona, Va., 1973.

Johnson, William. *Sketches of the Life and Correspondence of Nathanael Greene, Major General of the Armies of the United States in the War of the Revolution, Compiled Chiefly from Original Materials.* Charleston, S.C., 1822.

Kegley, Mary, and F.B. Kegley. *Early Adventures on the Western Waters.* 2 vols. Orange, Va., 1980.

Kincaid, Robert L. *The Wilderness Road.* Middlesboro, Ky., 1966.

Kleber, John E., ed. *The Kentucky Encyclopedia.* Lexington, Ky., 1992.

Lofaro, Michael A. *The Life and Adventures of Daniel Boone.* Lexington, Ky., 1978.

Mason, Kathryn Harrod. *James Harrod of Kentucky.* Baton Rouge, La., 1951.

Murray-Wooley, Carolyn. *The Founding of Lexington, 1775-1776.* Lexington, Ky., 1975.

O'Donnell, James H., III. *Southern Indians in the American Revolution.* Knoxville, Tenn., 1973.

Peck, John Mason. *Life of Daniel Boone, the Pioneer of Kentucky.* Boston, 1847.

Ranck, George W. *Boonesborough.* Louisville, Ky., 1901.

Rice, Otis K. *The Allegheny Frontier.* Lexington, Ky., 1970.

———. *Frontier Kentucky.* Lexington, Ky., 1975.

Rockenfield, Sarah Ridge. *Our Boone Families.* Evansville, Ind., 1987.

Spraker, Hazel Atterbury. *The Boone Family.* 2d ed. Baltimore, 1974.

Stevens, Frank E. *The Black Hawk War.* Chicago, 1903.

Stone, Richard G., Jr. *A Brittle Sword: The Kentucky Militia, 1776-1912.* Lexington, Ky., 1977.

Sword, Wiley. *President Washington's Indian War.* Norman, Okla., 1985.

Talbert, Charles Gano. *Benjamin Logan: Kentucky Frontiersman.* Lexington, Ky., 1962.

Taylor, Richard. *Girty.* Frankfort, Ky., 1977.

Thornely, Samuel, ed. *The Journal of Nicholas Cresswell, 1774-1777.* New York, 1924.

Thwaites, Reuben Gold, and Louise Phelps Kellogg. *Documentary History of Dunmore's War, 1774.* Madison, Wis., 1905.

Van Every, Dale. *A Company of Heroes.* New York, 1962.

Ward, Christopher. *The War of the Revolution.* 2 vols. New York, 1952.

Wrobel, Sylvia, and George Grider. *Isaac Shelby: Kentucky's First Governor and Hero of Three Wars.* Danville, Ky., 1973.

Young, Chester Raymond, ed. *Westward into Kentucky: The Narrative of Daniel Trabue.* Lexington, Ky., 1981.

Bibliography

Articles

Back, Francis. "The Canadian Capot." *Museum of the Fur Trade Quarterly* (fall 1991): 4-15.

Bate, R. Alexander. "Colonel Richard Callaway, 1722-1780." *Filson Club History Quarterly* 29 (Jan., Apr. 1955): 3-20, 166-178.

Beckner, Lucien. "John Findley: The First Pathfinder." *Filson Club History Quarterly* 43 (July 1969): 206-15.

Belue, Ted Franklin. "Chester Harding, James Otto Lewis, and Col. Daniel Boone." *Filson Club History Quarterly* 70 (Oct. 1996): 405-18.

———. "Did Daniel Boone Kill Pompey, the Black Shawnee, at the 1778 Siege of Boonesborough?" *Filson Club History Quarterly* 67 (Jan. 1993): 5-22.

———. "Olive's Gift," *Muzzleloader Magazine* (Mar. 1991): 58-61.

———. "Terror in the Canelands: The Fate of Daniel Boone's Salt Boilers." *Filson Club History Quarterly* 68 (Jan. 1994): 3-34.

Caywood, W.C., Jr. "Boone in Missouri: 1800-1820." *Filson Club History Quarterly* 38 (Apr. 1964): 115-24.

Haffner, Herald O. "Colonel Henry Hamilton, A Famous POW of the American Revolution." *Filson Club History Quarterly* 29 (Oct. 1955): 339-48.

Hagy, James William. "The First Attempt to Settle Kentucky: Boone in Virginia." *Filson Club History Quarterly* 44 (July 1970): 227-34.

Hall, Richard H. "Callaway Family Date." *Filson Club History Quarterly* 29 (Oct. 1955): 331-38.

Hammon, Neal O. "The First Trip to Boonesborough." *Filson Club History Quarterly* 45 (July 1971): 249-63.

———. "John Filson's Error." *Filson Club History Quarterly* 59 (Oct. 1985): 462-63.

———. "Legend of Daniel Boone's Cabin at Harrodsburg." *Filson Club History Quarterly* 48 (July 1974): 241-52.

Henderson, Archibald. "Transylvania Company Personnel." *Filson Club History Quarterly* 21 (Jan. 1947): 3-21.

Igleheart, Ted. "Squire Boone, the Forgotten Man." *Filson Club History Quarterly* 44 (Oct. 1970): 357-66.

McChesney, H.V., ed. "Certificate Book of the Virginia Land Commission of 1779-80." *Register of the Kentucky Historical Society* 21 (1923): 1-321.

Meese, William E. "Credit Island, 1814-1914." *Journal of the Illinois State Historical Society* 7 (Jan. 1915): 349-73.

Talbert, Charles G. "A Roof for Kentucky." *Filson Club History Quarterly* 29 (Apr. 1955): 145-62.

Bibliography

Documents

Draper, Lyman Copeland. Manuscripts. State Historical Society of Wisconsin,
McKee, Alexander, to Major De Peyster, August 28, 1782. Colonial Office
Records, series 2, vol. 20, p. 288. Reports of the Public Archives of Canada,
Canadian Archives, Ottawa.
Mayfield, R.N., M.D. "Boone Family History." Filson Club, 1945. Typescript.
Stevens, Frank E. "Illinois in the War of 1812-4; Transactions of the Illinois
State Historical Society." Springfield, Ill., 1904.

INDEX

Index

Index

NATHAN BOONE FAMILY

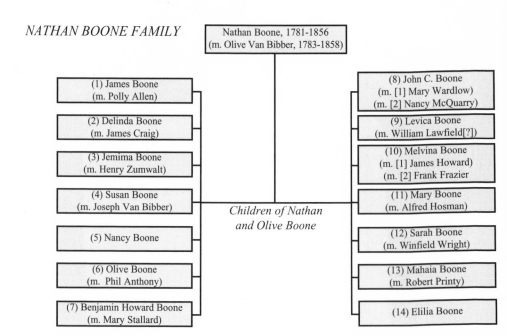

Nathan Boone, 1781-1856
(m. Olive Van Bibber, 1783-1858)

*Children of Nathan
and Olive Boone*

(1) James Boone
(m. Polly Allen)

(2) Delinda Boone
(m. James Craig)

(3) Jemima Boone
(m. Henry Zumwalt)

(4) Susan Boone
(m. Joseph Van Bibber)

(5) Nancy Boone

(6) Olive Boone
(m. Phil Anthony)

(7) Benjamin Howard Boone
(m. Mary Stallard)

(8) John C. Boone
(m. [1] Mary Wardlow)
(m. [2] Nancy McQuarry)

(9) Levica Boone
(m. William Lawfield[?])

(10) Melvina Boone
(m. [1] James Howard)
(m. [2] Frank Frazier

(11) Mary Boone
(m. Alfred Hosman)

(12) Sarah Boone
(m. Winfield Wright)

(13) Mahaia Boone
(m. Robert Printy)

(14) Elilia Boone

CALLAWAY FAMILY

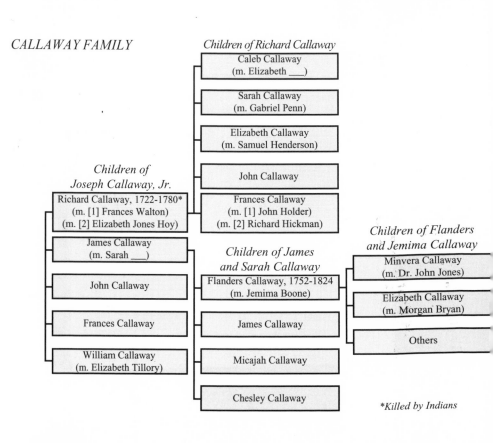

*Children of
Joseph Callaway, Jr.*

Richard Callaway, 1722-1780*
(m. [1] Frances Walton)
(m. [2] Elizabeth Jones Hoy)

James Callaway
(m. Sarah ___)

John Callaway

Frances Callaway

William Callaway
(m. Elizabeth Tillory)

Children of Richard Callaway

Caleb Callaway
(m. Elizabeth ___)

Sarah Callaway
(m. Gabriel Penn)

Elizabeth Callaway
(m. Samuel Henderson)

John Callaway

Frances Callaway
(m. [1] John Holder)
(m. [2] Richard Hickman)

*Children of James
and Sarah Callaway*

Flanders Callaway, 1752-1824
(m. Jemima Boone)

James Callaway

Micajah Callaway

Chesley Callaway

*Children of Flanders
and Jemima Callaway*

Minvera Callaway
(m. Dr. John Jones)

Elizabeth Callaway
(m. Morgan Bryan)

Others

Killed by Indians